ALLIED DUNBAR LIBRARY
MONEY GUIDES

RUNNING YOUR OWN BUSINESS

Second Edition

RUNNING YOUR OWN BUSINESS

DAVID WILLIAMS

Second Edition

Foreword by

HRH The Prince of Wales

© Allied Dunbar Financial Services Limited 1990

ISBN 0-85121-651X

Published by

Longman Law, Tax and Finance
Longman Group UK Limited
21–27 Lamb's Conduit Street, London WC1N 3NJ

Associated Offices

Australia, Hong Kong, Malaysia, Singapore, USA

A CIP catalogue record for this book is available from the British Library.

Printed in Great Britain by
Biddles Ltd, Guildford and King's Lynn

David Williams

David Williams is qualified both as a solicitor and a tax adviser. He has written and lectured widely on both law and taxation for over a decade. Amongst his other works are **Tax for the Self-Employed** and **Making Your Job Work** both Allied Dunbar Money Guides published by Longman, and practitioners' and students' books on tax, administrative law and social security law, as well as other books and regular contributions to journals and newspapers. He is the consultant editor of the Reader's Digest guide to the law, **You and your Rights**, and for several years appeared on and was a legal adviser to Granada Television's community advice programme **This is your Right**. He currently also holds a senior post sponsored by Price Waterhouse, one of the world's leading accountancy firms, in the **Centre for Commercial Law Studies**, Queen Mary College, University of London.

KENSINGTON PALACE

The aims of the Prince's Youth Business Trust are straightforward – it exists to encourage the enterprise and skill of thousands of young people all over the country who may otherwise remain unemployed and unable to find the support necessary to start off in a business.

The demand for the Trust's services has been greater than was ever imagined and this in turn has put considerable pressure on its resources. It has therefore been enormously encouraging to see the level of support and contributions provided by the many individuals, companies and organisations which ensure that the Trust can fulfil its commitments. Its success can best be demonstrated by results. Over 20,000 young people have received advice; over 9,000 of them have received loans and grants. 8 out of 10 of those who have received support for their business ideas are trading successfully after the first year.

Towards the end of 1987 the Trust launched a major appeal for substantial funds to enable it to expand its activities. Support is coming in many different ways – and the sponsorship of this book is one of them.

I welcome its publication for two reasons. Firstly, because of the guidance and advice that would-be entrepreneurs will get from it and secondly, because of the contribution its sales will make to the continued availability of financial help to the next generation.

The Prince's Youth Business Trust

The Prince's Youth Business Trust was formed by the merger of the Youth Enterprise Scheme and the Youth Business Initiative in 1986. These two organisations came together to form the single largest private sector initiative in the UK to help young people to set up and run their own businesses. Established as a charitable trust, PYBT provides a comprehensive range of seedcorn finance, business advice and information, enterprise training and marketing support.

In conjunction with Business in the Community, the Trust is developing a number of Business Centres through which a wide range of services related to youth employment are offered.

Initial funding for the Trust was provided by the Royal Jubilee Trusts and the Prince's Trust, with Investors In Industry subsequently making available an interest free loan of £½m. Industry and commerce contribute through the Business Bursary Scheme and a number of charitable trusts help with finance, as do some local authorities. Donations in kind are provided by many companies and local authorities particularly in the form of accommodation, support services and equipment. The Chairman and members of all Regional Boards (some 500 people in all) and some 3,000 Business Advisors give their services to the Trust on an entirely voluntary basis.

The Trust launched an appeal at the end of 1987 to raise £40 million to develop its activities. To achieve this the Trust is talking to companies, charitable trusts, local Government, and private individuals, seeking donations out of marketing and sponsorship budgets as well as charitable gifts. To help in this appeal, the Government has announced that, until April 1990, it will double the amount of donations being received from the private sector.

The Allied Dunbar Group will be donating their proceeds of this book to the Trust.

Introduction

Now is the enterprise age. Surveys show that there has been a rapid rise in recent years in the number of active small businesses. Other surveys show that there are also many people who, given the right opportunities or ideas, would like to join those who are going it alone. Sometimes they · hesitate because they are not sure how to go about it.

Governments for over a decade past have eased the way of smaller businesses. Taxes on small businesses have been reduced, as has form-filling and various bureaucratic requirements. More positively, facilities and advice have been made more readily available both by government and by business itself – and there has grown up a whole range of advice and counselling for the new or growing business. As this book was written, this was being emphasised by the government's Enterprise Initiative. But a lot of important questions still remain for anyone venturing into his or her own business.

Where do you start? What points should be watched? How much money is needed and when? What legal requirements must be met? Should you set up as a company or a partnership? Where can you turn for help? How do you go about finding premises? Is a franchise a good idea? Is your idea of a new product a sound one which will sell well? All sorts of questions like these will, or should, come to mind. Some of these questions this book, or those this book advises you to consult, can handle for you. Some you alone can answer.

Where this book and the advice sources it details can help, even in those areas it or they cannot answer for you, is to make sure you know the questions that should be asked, and set the right way about getting the answers. If you get your planning right and get the right advice on the more tricky questions, your chances of making your new business a success will be very much greater. Many have in recent years started their own thriving businesses. Theirs is the dream of making a success of what they do. It is a dream many seek – and many can achieve, if their approach is positive. If it is your dream, you are right to hesitate, but you can seek to answer your doubts right now.

Contents

1 Getting started . . .

That's easy. You already have. If not before, you started when you opened this book.

Like everyone else running or intending to run their own business, you have lots of questions needing answers before you really get going. There will be still more questions later. That's the reason for this book. It will help you ask the right questions, and set about getting the right answers. It will help you think about the problems confronting your business in a way that allows you to read through quickly whilst thinking generally, but then to come back to the areas on which you need or wish to spend more time when making your plans more definite. And it will help you set about getting advice from the right experts.

To help you work through your questions, and the answers to them, you need a pencil and some paper. So, before we go any further, go and get yourself a suitable sharp pencil, some sheets of paper or a notebook and, if you wish, a rubber too. Only when you have them should you turn the page.

You've found the pencil! Good. You'll need it quite a lot in order to plan your business properly.

The aims of this book

Its first aim is to encourage you to look at yourself and assess why you want to run your own business (Chapter 2). It then answers questions about how you start a business and the forms it might take (Chapters 3 to 5). Next, it aims to help you think through and plan all the important aspects of your business – the five Ps: Purpose, Product, Potential, People, Pounds. The importance of this plan is emphasised in Chapter 6, and Chapters 7 to 15 look in detail at what is involved: products and how to market them, how to raise and control cash, how to employ others. Finally, we look at the next stage, growing bigger (Chapter 16). Why not have a quick look through before we get going, so you can see what's ahead. There is a useful list of addresses at the end.

The book tells you what planning and research you must carry out, and the decisions you must take, and also tells you when to get the experts in, and how to get the best from the free and subsidised advisory services available in most areas.

And for those who didn't get a pencil . . .

. . . ask yourself why. A management school sets all its candidates for entry a written examination. Candidates are told to turn up to the exam room armed with two sharp 2B pencils, a rubber and a ruler – and nothing else. As they enter the exam room, candidates are asked to show their equipment. Anyone who does not have exactly the equipment they were asked to bring is not allowed in to the exam room. They are excluded from, and have therefore failed, the exam. Why?

There is one brutal little lesson they have learned. The exam began long before they thought it did. They expected the questions to start when the three-hour session started, but no one else told them that – they had jumped to the wrong conclusion and had only themselves to blame for not taking notice of the advice and instructions.

Bearing in mind your business has also started, a pencil would be a very good idea. Keep it by you and write notes as you go along. Now, on to the next page and we'll really get down to business.

2 Starting on your own

Let's begin at the beginning. There is one thing in common
to your plans – or rather a whole series of things in common
– whatever you choose to do. It's **you**, and your strengths
and weaknesses, and it's with you we must start. People go
into business for a whole series of different reasons, some out
of complete choice, others because they feel they have no
other choice. The DTI recently estimated that the net number
of businesses had increased at an average of 500 a week since
1979. A survey at the same time showed that a large number
of managers who were employees wanted to break out on
their own, for a variety of reasons. What are your reasons?

You've got a good idea?

Many employees, whilst working away at their jobs, realise
they could be doing the same thing for themselves better
and more profitably than their employer. Or perhaps they
could be running the whole business better than their
employer. There have been many successful examples of
management buy-outs in recent years. Even on a small scale
it can work very well. If you really do know your job, and
you see a niche in the market and customers for your new
product or service, you may well be in a strong position. But
think it through thoroughly before you jump in.

Choosing your career?

Self-employment is readily forgotten when people leaving school or college think about what they want to do. It's quite easy for the armed forces, wealthy businesses like banks, or glamour industries like airlines to mount impressive displays at local careers conventions. Putting up an attractive display for 'the self-employed' is not so easy, because it covers so many different things. Our society has been used over many years to others supplying our job opportunities for us, perhaps too used to it. This is not so of some of our minority communities, whose backgrounds make them more ready to set up their own businesses. Choice of career is partly an attitude of mind, and the more open it is the better.

There is help and advice available especially for the young as we shall see later, and there are ways you can explore this choice of career just as thoroughly as any other. You'd be wrong to dismiss it as an option if you're the right kind of person.

Redundant?

In recent years many people have experienced the nasty shock of redundancy, often through no fault of their own. They were, they thought, safely employed in a secure job until they learned one day that very few jobs are really secure, and theirs wasn't one of them. All too soon, they were unemployed, perhaps with some redundancy money, perhaps not. There are several schemes, and financial help, if this is what has happened to you.

Over the last few years literally millions of people have found themselves redundant. Some have found other employment but many have not. Some have used the chance to make good again on their own, sometimes with the active help of their former employer. In the last few years there has been a marked increase in help for all self-employed people, and for this group in particular. Help and advice are available, especially right at the beginning, and this book explains where.

Fed up with your job?

Many other people still in work are thoroughly fed up with what they are now doing. Though they didn't at first realise, their life was like being on a conveyor belt or production line. They are put on it by their parents. At the age of five it was off to school, which shunted them on for the next ten years or so. Then perhaps off to college or on to a job suggested to them, or where their friends went, or perhaps it was to the only employer with jobs at the time.

One day the conveyor belt stops. Suddenly they realise that they want to run their own lives, but the experience is a new one to them, and they want to know what to do next. If that describes you, then you are right to be reading this book because before you do anything else, you need to think, and then plan. I have seen all too many people decide one day they can't stand their job any longer, and just walk out.

Only afterwards they discover that their employer is quite happy to see them go, and stops their pay there and then. But the Social Security Office isn't, and they get hardly any state benefit, and before long they're almost completely out of money. Their friends find it very puzzling, and the family start grumbling. They have no idea what to do next, and no one else seems interested. Make sure you always think about what to do next.

Want to be your own boss?

Perhaps you are looking for the challenge of living on your wits, without the constraints of others asking what you are doing, and demanding your explanations for what is, or should be, happening? Your wish may be to be independent, not just of being told what to do, but of other people's way of thinking about things and doing things. You want the satisfaction of getting it right yourself.

These are just some of the reasons why people become self-employed. With over 10,000 extra businesses officially started in 1989, and the number of self-employed now estimated to be 3 million, there are likely to be a lot of others. Your reasons may be totally different to all those above, or maybe there are a mixture of reasons. What are *your* reasons?

Get your pencil, and write out your answers to these two questions:

I want to run my own business because

....

....

....

....

....

I think I will be good at it because

....

....

....

....

....

Were you expecting the second question? Are you happy with the answer you have given to the question? Is it a good answer? Perhaps those are unfair questions. What does being 'good' at running a business involve? That is, of course, what much of this book is about and we're only on page 8 at the moment!

The question is a crucial one because not everyone is the right sort of person to be self-employed. Some are 'naturals' at it, whilst many others can get there with hard work. One thing is for sure. You need, in the words of the philosopher, to 'know thyself' before you start. You can fool me with the answers you give – but don't fool yourself. Let's look at the strengths and weaknesses you possess.

What was your last job?

The best place to start is with what you are now doing, or were last doing when at work. What were the good and bad sides of that work? In particular, if you are thinking of giving up a job, what is it about the job that you can't stick? Is it a personality clash with the boss or your fellow staff? If so, is it their fault or yours? If it's your fault, how will becoming self-employed help? In what ways were you good at that job, and what parts did you find difficult? Much as you would like to start from somewhere else, you can't.

Those are all questions designed to make you think about the real you, because it's you that you're going to have to work with all the time in your new business. As a help, I've set out a list of questions and points below. Think about each point carefully. It may help to write notes beside each question as you go along. And remember, be honest. You owe it to yourself.

The right answers?

There is no one right answer to all these questions, except that if you cannot say 'yes' to the question about believing in yourself then you really do need to think very hard before you go any further. After all, if you do not have confidence in your own abilities, how can anyone else be expected to take you seriously? You can tell, can't you, within a minute of meeting people for the first time whether they are self-confident. Equally, other people will judge you just as quickly, and just as firmly.

Your state of health will matter more for some jobs than others – indeed some people fighting serious disabilities find one way of doing it is through self-employment in an appropriate area of work. If that applies to you, you can get special help from a number of sources (see Chapter 4, 'Get the experts in').

While particular demands of different businesses mean that the same answers are not needed to all the questions, people who are best at self-employment are people possessing more than average of some special qualities. They need lots of energy and confidence, a more than average amount of self-reliance and a clear awareness of their own strengths and weaknesses. Above all, they need the **'bounce back factor'**,

Checklist: What are my strengths?

Personality

- How tough are you? If the going gets rough will you stick it out? Did you, last time you hit a problem?
- Are you a self-starter? Do you motivate yourself, or do you need others to give you the ideas or example?
- Are you prepared to take decisions, especially hard ones? And not blame others if you get it wrong?
- Did you take responsibility last time you made a mistake, or is it always someone else's fault?
- Are you good at organising yourself or other people?

Health

- How good are you at coping with stress and strain?
- Can you work long hours without collapsing in a heap?
- Can you survive without holidays, and losing your weekends, if the business needs your time?
- How many times have you been ill in the last few years? Are those problems going to recur?
- What would your doctor say about you taking on your own business? Should you ask him or her?

Dealing with other people

- How well do you get on with other people socially? Do you have many friends and contacts?
- How well do you get on with others at work? Are you a good leader at work, on the sports field, at the local youth club, anywhere?
- Are you good at taking advice from others?
- Are you the sort of person people rely on, or do you tend to rely on others?

Self-confidence

- Do you believe in yourself, and have confidence in your own abilities and decisions?

Experience

- What training and qualifications do you have for the business you want to run?
- What work experience do you have of that kind of business?
- Are you experienced in managing your own time and money, or that of other people?

a mixture of energy, confidence, willpower, persistence, self-reliance, even courage. It is the ability to take knocks and blows and not give up – to still be in the action when others have retired from it. How far do you have those abilities?

What your family think

Although most people think they know themselves well, they are not always the best people to answer questions about themselves. Their immediate family and close friends often know how they will behave as well as, and sometimes better than, they do. What do your family and your friends think of your ideas?

Getting your family behind what you are doing is particularly important. Research shows that those who start their own businesses with their family behind them are much more likely to succeed that those who do not – as much as four times as likely. Even better, as we shall discuss later, if the family are prepared to help do the work.

If you are a family man or woman you owe it to your family to take their views fully into account. It is their livelihood and, often, home which is at risk as well as yours. And if they are on your side, they can be tremendous allies. Perhaps your wife or husband ought to be your partner in your new business, and not just a supporter or part-time employee.

And your friends

Similarly, your friends can be of enormous value – again, maybe the business would be better run by two or more partners, even if some are only part-time. They can help you find customers and ideas – or they can tell you (but often won't unless you ask them to be absolutely honest) that they think the idea is wrong.

What do you think now?

What does all this self-questioning tell you? I do not know, but you do. If you do have that 'bounce back factor' and your family and friends are right behind you, then we need to take your plans very seriously. But if what all this tells you is that your dream ought to remain just that, then you have not wasted your time. You know your future should lie elsewhere. If in spite of that information, you still go ahead, you may be making a serious mistake. Now is the time to reframe your plans and start on surer ground.

If you think I'm being very negative, you are absolutely right! Why? I'm not trying to put you off becoming self-employed if you know what you are doing. I am trying, rather, to make sure you stop and think before you commit yourself, because many before you have not done so.

Every year, a considerable number of small businesses fail completely and cease business. A much greater number – well over half – will fail to provide the high levels of material wealth some seek in their own business. By no means all of those are failures. Some stay small because that is what the people running them want. Their objectives are different. Perhaps yours are too. How did you answer the questions at the beginning of this section? Other businesses were meant to be bigger but did not make it. In some of these cases it is for the most basic reason: the person running the business was not up to it. Two other basic reasons are a failure to plan and a failure to take proper advice. You have been warned!

What kind of business?

You probably have some idea of the kind of business you aim to pursue. Even so, you still need to think very hard about how you are going to use your skills, inventions or ideas in your business. If you are not already tied to exploiting a particular line of business, your choice should be a matter of careful thought. Try and identify areas of activity that make the fullest use of your skills, abilities and material resources, so that you start as far along the road to success as you can.

If you are short of ideas or want to check them out, you can start right in your own home with the *Yellow Pages* telephone book. Look for all the different kinds of business there are, and how many other people are already exploiting your idea in your locality. Between Abattoirs and Zoos in my local directory are 25 pages full of ideas. You can chase an idea further by a visit to your nearest commercial library. There is one in every big town or city; your local library will tell you where the nearest one is. That will have a whole series of trade journals and directories to help you.

Goods and services

We can break up different kinds of businesses usefully into three broad groupings.

Creating goods – This means either setting up a factory unit to produce your goods, or being a manufacturer in the old sense (the word meant make by hand!) creating individual items of art or craft: clothing, furniture, toys, sculpture. In each case you must have (or buy) the necessary artistic or engineering skills. In most cases, you also need a fair amount of cash right at the beginning, to buy premises and equipment. What is more, that money will be tied permanently into the business.

Buying and selling goods – At first glance, this is the most open of the three groupings. Everyone has some experience of buying and selling – or at least of buying. They may think they do not need much expertise to get involved in many areas of selling. Is that really so? The life of many small shopkeepers is tough, as the competition of the big superstores and multiple chains steadily erodes their potential share of the market. Here again it is often the people with special skills that do best – though it may be easier to acquire some of those skills, and there are always gaps in what is sold locally. Even so, you still need money that can be tied up in the stock and premises.

Providing services – This is the growth area of the British economy over recent years, especially in such areas as tourism, convenience services (such as fast food), leisure facilities and financial services. Look how the High Streets of most towns have changed over the last ten years. Again, the big organisations have muscled in, but there are still plenty of opportunities to be found, some involving much less initial capital. Often they are services to the big organisations which they find it better to sub-contract out than do in-house.

Which kind of activity are you considering? It should be one that provides a genuine business opportunity, not a passing fashion or work only for a short period. It should be one that uses to the full your own skills and strengths, and resorts less to those areas in which you are not skilled. And it should be properly affordable for you. Organising your approach to any of these areas is discussed later in the book. But there are some provisional exercises you can do right now with your idea.

The ten year test

Take a sheet of paper and write on it what you think will
have happened to your area of business ten years from now,
regardless of whether you succeed or fail. It's not impossible
– Government and big industry employ people to do just
this. For example, how will the make-up of the local
community have changed? If the prices of houses locally are
pricing out the youngsters with local jobs, what will the
community be like in a few years' time? Let's have a look
at what those changes might be.

How things will change

In most areas there will be more elderly people – over 100,000
more in the whole country in the next three years. There will
be fewer people leaving school and in their young twenties,
but there will be more children of younger school age,
though this will vary from area to area. New houses bought
by young couples will, in ten years, have children in them.
At the same time, slightly older estates that now have lots of
children in them may, ten years on, have seen most of them
leave home, and the local schools a lot emptier. Other, subtler,
changes are occurring because of the price of housing and
the increasing mobility of the population. People are less
integrated and more separated, eg, into middle class areas,
than once was the case. They travel more and have a wider
experience of, and often also expectations of, life.

The job market

There will be more people retiring from work than coming into the labour market for the first time, so there will be shortages of skilled workers, particularly professionals, in a few years time (indeed the shortage is already happening in some areas). Some businesses and professions are already worried about that. How many children will be leaving school or college in your area in each of the next few years? The schools know that. Should you? How will work patterns have changed in ten years? Will the shift towards part-time employment and people working from their own homes continue – made far more possible by computers, faxes and the other inventions of information technology?

How people behave

People will be healthier and have more leisure time. They will probably smoke and drink less, and eat better food. They will still be retiring younger, but will be living longer. But will all this spare time, and the 'spare' time of the unemployed and underemployed, mean that the crime rate goes on climbing as it has done in recent years? If so, how will people react to that? What else will people do with their leisure? Will the promise of still cheaper air travel mean that everyone has three holidays abroad, where not so long ago they had one week at Blackpool?

Wealthier people (and for this purpose I mean most of us – the majority of households who own their own homes) will get wealthier. This is because, for the first time, as older people die, they leave their increasingly valuable homes to their families. But, unlike previous generations, those families also already own their own homes. Will they use their second home as a holiday home, or rent it out, or sell it and reinvest the money in something else – either savings or higher consumer spending? Again, serious study of the effects of this shift is already going on. It is assumed that the result in part will be greatly increased savings. Where will the savings go?

What will happen in your area?

These things are not guesswork. We already know they are going to happen, as the inevitable consequence (catastrophes apart) of the present way the population is made up in different parts of the country, and the effects in the future of new discoveries and practices.

With a bit of detective work, you can do a lot more guessing about the future in your area. If there is a new motorway or road improvement planned, what will its effect be when it is opened? The effect of the M25, or of the electrification of lines into Liverpool Street Station, has been enormous in those areas. So is the growth of Manchester International Airport, which went on growing even when some tried to stop it. And it will go on growing. What opportunities will that provide?

And what of the Channel Tunnel, and the planned removal of internal barriers in the European Community in 1993? On the other hand, the number of people employed on the land in ordinary farming activities is still dropping, and now forms a negligible, but still over-producing, sector of a country that, not so long ago, was a land of farmers. The same is true of mining, shipbuilding and steel, so the towns that used to depend on these businesses are still declining. This process is now being accelerated as the world goes 'green'. Increasing awareness of environment and the need to care for it will have a profound influence on all our futures. But how?

Hi-tech and low-tech

Think what technology is doing. Take this book, for example. It was written on a hard-disk word processor, with a memory big enough to store the whole of this and several other books. When I started writing books, it was with a manual typewriter. The change in the technology of writing and publishing is enormous, and that's just one small part of the information technology revolution.

Don't get too fascinated by hi-tech, though. Many of the inventions that have affected us most are more low-tech, like cling-wrap and plastic bags, cassette players and car parts that don't need servicing every three weeks. I've said enough to make my point. There should be quite a lot you can already put down on paper. Once we have looked at the information available to you elsewhere (see Chapter 8, 'What are you selling?') there will be much more.

Think as an entrepreneur

Why? Entrepreneurs are innovators. They are the people who spot, or as often as not create, new markets and new customers. Just think what is on the market now that was not available ten years ago. Who put it there? Many of these developments involve very little new – what's new in a hamburger this century? Nor was the work done by the inventor – as British history sadly shows time and again. Rather, someone else came along and persuaded us we needed this 'new' product, to his benefit.

Quite often, these people were the ones who sat down and thought through the changes that were about to take place in their business, or sometimes the changes that should have taken place, but had not.

Sometimes it is all too obvious. As small shops have given way to large shops, so stores have been staffed, in their customers' views, either by no one at all or by shop assistants who either ignore or are rude to the customers. Big has meant anonymous. Many people like a friendly shop. Hence a belated move to get staff in big stores to be as friendly as they always were in the successful local store. The stores where assistants were recruited and trained to help the customer, where they don't mind you bringing the clothes back if they don't fit, are doing well, aren't they?

Sometimes, on a much smaller scale, the entrepreneur is the one who spotted a gap in the local market for a product or service and supplied it, and did it so well that whilst there are a lot of customers for his goods or services, he can compete successfully enough not to make it worth anyone else's while to compete with him. Our local specialist cheese shop is like that – and every Saturday morning there is a queue out through the door despite the speed at which his four assistants work.

Where do you come in?

The kind of business or opportunity you seize should make the most of your strengths and available resources. But it should also be one that suits the lifestyle you want to lead. What kind of commitment do you want to make to your business? In terms of both time and training this may vary enormously. Think of the different hours kept by offices and shops in your own locality. There are sedate offices which only keep 'office hours' – which seems to mean hardly any at all in some cases. And there are the corner shops that are always open. Consider the hours worked by the manager of your local pub – or the time in the morning when the local newsagent or greengrocer start work.

If you are willing to be committed to a business for those

hours, you have a valuable asset at your disposal. If not, you may be planning self-imposed imprisonment. Again, the demands during the day will vary enormously. The newsagent's work is largely done by the time the rest of us emerge, until the evening newsround. The launderette, on the other hand, needs to be open all day every day, but only needs close attention when there are problems. Those prepared to offer emergency services – for which premium prices will be paid – need constantly to be ready, but will be paid well for it.

What else do you do?

A lot of people consider working on their own to fit in with other all-consuming interests: sports activities, art or music, or something else which by itself will not earn a living. If that is what you are planning, think about the varying demands of the business you choose through the week and year. How does that fit in with your other plans? Most businesses are seasonal, just as are most hobbies. Do the two go together? There is a season for just about everything, from toymakers and toyshops (which have to make their profits in the hectic scramble before Christmas) to building – which is always slackest when the toyshops are at their busiest.

Taking the plunge

Even when you know your own strengths and weaknesses, and have an area of business in mind, there is still much more to think about. The main thing you need to do is to work out your business plan. At the same time, you need to be thinking how best you can start in the business.

Part-timing

One point meriting immediate thought is whether you start your new venture whole-time or part-time. Can you start your business in the evenings and weekends, keeping your main job going until you do not need it any more? This is worth considering even more when the venture is a family venture. Can one of you keep working (or start work at a reliable job) whilst the other one works at the business? And you don't have to keep on your present job to do this – there may well be other less demanding opportunities around.

Keeping a regular source of income going whilst you get started on your own business makes a lot of sense, if you can do it. There will be no need for quite the same desperate panic if your new venture is slower getting off the ground than you thought. And if your new venture proves to be a mistake, you still have another source of revenue to fall back on. How far you can do this varies from one business to another, as in some businesses you need to devote your whole time and effort from the beginning if it is going to be a success.

Many successful small businesses were started really small, and only became full-time businesses when the work warranted it. Others will, or should, expect always to remain so unless they are unusually successful. This is particularly true of the arts and craft industries, where customers are notoriously reluctant to pay the real going rate for a painting or hand-crafted toy or furniture.

Combining two jobs has become much easier in recent years. Hours of full-time jobs in many sectors of the economy have become shorter, with less compulsory overtime being worked. There are also many more part-time jobs available in the labour market, also opportunities to job-share. At the same time, flexibility of work has increased considerably.

There is another side to this story. In some areas of business, you need to be available all the time right from the start. Customers will not wait when you ask them to, they will go off to your competitors. And you may find it very hard to get your business going whilst at the same time having to direct even a little of your attention to keeping your boss quiet.

Enterprise Allowance

If you are not in employment, and do not find any suitable work, other help is available for you under the Government's Enterprise Allowance Scheme. There are over 100,000 places available for those who qualify. Each pays £40 a week for a year to those who are on unemployment benefit or income support to help them get started on their new job. Otherwise, if they start work, they lose social security entitlement immediately.

If you want to claim Enterprise Allowance, check with your local Jobcentre. You will be asked to attend an Awareness Day, at which some of the things discussed in this book will be raised. You will have to show you meet the following conditions:

- you are receiving unemployment benefit or income support
- you have been unemployed for 13 weeks
- you have not yet started in self-employment
- you intend, when you do start, to work full-time at your new business
- you must show that the idea is one appropriate for Government support
- you must be 18 or over and below pensionable age
- you must be able to raise £1,000 either from your own resources, or as a small business loan. To find out more, get the **Enterprise Allowance guide** from your Jobcentre.

Apart from weekly payments, you will be offered chances to take part in training courses for small businesses, and probably be offered counselling help. Even if it is not offered direct, it is available, as we see below.

Another key question as you start planning is whether you should start your business right from scratch, or should buy an existing business, or should join a franchise or similar organisation where some of the work is done for you. You need to decide what kind of structure your business has – partnership, cooperative, company or sole trader. An important issue in those decisions is whether you become self-employed on your own (as we have assumed so far, so we concentrate on you) or together with one or more others. These alternatives are the subject of the next two Chapters.

The Prince's Youth Business Trust

The Trust provides professional advice, test marketing support, business training and work experience for young people who are unemployed or disadvantaged in some way. It also encourages people in creating their own jobs and to develop their entrepreneurial talents.

Some 3,000 Business Advisers operate from a network of regional centres, to provide advice to the young in starting up in business. A list of telephone numbers is given at the end of this book. The Trust also provides non-refundable bursaries and low-interest loans to help get businesses started.

The way the Trust works is explained in more detail in Chapter 4, 'Help for the young'.

3 Buying a business

If you do not wish to start from scratch, you can get into business in two ways. You can buy an existing concern, stepping into the shoes of the previous owner. Alternatively, you can buy your way into a franchise operation, where some parts of the business will come ready made, whilst other parts will be for you to start for yourself. Either way, you need to make thorough initial enquiries before agreeing to go ahead.

Buying an existing business

When buying, or buying into, an existing business, you are purchasing several different things at once, each demanding separate thought. Included are:

- **Premises** – Does the business own or lease its premises? Is living accommodation included? Will you be using this or letting it? What are the rates and other outgoings like?
- **Fixed assets** – Is the business well or poorly equipped? What are you paying for this equipment, and what are you going to have to pay out to replace it or maintain it?
- **Trading stock** – Is the business well stocked, overstocked, stocked with obsolete goods?
- **Knowhow** – Do you need any specialist knowledge to run the business? If so, are you buying it? Do you need to buy or obtain any licence rights to any intellectual property, that is, copyrights, trade marks, patents of inventions, or registered designs?
- **Goodwill** – This is payment for the intangible 'extras'

that go with any good business by way of contacts with customers, established trading record, and so on.

- *An order book* – of uncompleted and outstanding commitments of the business, and work in progress at the date you buy.
- *The business accounts* – Are you buying the company's debts as well, and any rights to be paid by current creditors? If so, what is the total liability and likely amount you will collect reasonably quickly?
- *Protective covenants* – Will the seller promptly open a new business round the corner in competition with yours? How can you stop him? Will he enter a non-competition covenant?

Be sure you are buying with your business all the aspects of it that you need to buy, and that you are paying a proper price for each part. To make sure of that, you need both to do some checking, and to get the experts in to help you. It is very tempting to do neither, especially if you think you have found a bargain. All too many people buy houses faster than they would buy a new vacuum cleaner. They assure themselves that if they don't like it, they can move again in a couple of years. Even for a householder, that is a waste of several thousand pounds (though I know quite a few who have done it). For a business, that may mean serious problems.

Check the market

Look around well before buying. Get preliminary details about as many businesses as you can. This will give you an idea of the right level of price, and of the sort of opportunities going. You will find details in the local newspapers, in *Daltons Weekly* or *Exchange and Mart*, or through local business transfer agents or estate agents who handle business sales. We'll take one from my local paper recently:

> **Easily run cut flowers/
> pot plant business**, with
> sales of quality confectionery.
> Excellent potential to introduce
> floristry. T/O £800/£1000 weekly
> on high GP margin. Most attractive
> s/shop on lease in centre of market
> town. £25,000 SAV.

Let's translate this into English. The offer is of a business combining some aspects of a florists shop with some aspects of a confectioners/sweetshop. It could be a florist's shop. Why isn't it? Our shop is on a lease (how long? how much rent? what chances of being thrown out of the tenancy?) in a town centre (how big is the town? how big is its centre?). The price is £25,000 plus stock at valuation. Borrowing at a cheap 10%, that means £2,500 to £3,000 interest (as well as rent) a year. This will earn us on their figures (being cautious) £40,000 a year, producing a gross profit of, say 40%, or £16,000. That leaves £13,500 after paying the mortgage, or nominal interest on capital, from which other expenses have to be deducted, such as rent, rates and staff costs if we employ any. If we do not, how much an hour will that return us for our efforts? But if the interest rate is 15%, then what?

To be sure, when we go along to the business transfer agent for the particulars, we will get rather a different story, and our description will seem very mean. They will give a much more positive account. But, as someone once said, they would, wouldn't they? They are, after all, on a no sale, no commission deal (it said so at the bottom of the ad), and they do not want their time wasted.

Questions to be asked

If this proposition interests you, what should you do? First, look around. Are there any similar businesses for sale elsewhere, especially in that town? Is the price a fair one by comparison? To answer that, you will need to know quite a bit more.

Why is the business being sold? The advertisement or the agent may say 'ceased partnership forces sale' or 'owner emigrating'. Why? Did one partner get fed up with the low profit margin, and is the owner emigrating to escape creditors?

Ask for the audited accounts of the business not just for the last year, but for the last five years or so. If the recent figures are 'being audited', then ask for provisional figures. Ideally, these should be handed straight to your accountant – and this is strongly recommended if you are seriously going ahead. But there are some interesting things you can easily learn yourself from those accounts.

What accounts can tell you

Seemingly innocent figures can tell you a great deal about the business, particularly if you can compare a series of years. In the last year, with a bit of creative accounting, some hard work, an extra effort to increase turnover and collect overdue bills (combined with a judicious slowness in paying bills out) a competent bookkeeper can work a few miracles. But it will not be kept up. Don't be fooled by the argument that the rest of the figures are concealed because they were not passed through the till. There will, in the nature of things, be no proof of that. What is more, whilst that might be true two or three years before the sale, the previous owner is much more likely to have passed everything through the accounts in the lead-up to the sale to get the audited figures as high as possible.

There is a full set of accounts in Chapter 12 'Control your money'. As an exercise, try the following tests out on those accounts. Would you like to buy Wibble Widgets, and if so, at what price?

Financial soundness

In addition to your own calculations of how much you have to borrow to buy into the business, you need to know how sound the business is. You, and anyone from whom you wish to borrow, should watch the *current ratio*. This is the ratio:

current assets: current liabilities

These figures are found on the balance sheet. What the ratio shows is how readily the business can pay its current debts. If the figures are near to or less than 1:1, then there are signs of potential trouble.

What if you suddenly had to pay all the debts (eg the overdraft was called in)? Could you sell all the stock at its balance sheet valuation? Probably not. For this reason, there is an even tighter ratio to watch, the *liquidity ratio* or *acid test*. This is:

current assets less stock: current liabilities

In other words, forgetting about the stock, how much money is there to meet all current creditors? If that ratio is strongly adverse, where does the money come from to meet the money owing to the creditors if they start pushing for payment?

A low ratio may suggest that there is too much short term credit in the business, whilst a very high ratio suggests that there is a good reserve of long term credit or owner's capital. Looked at another way, a bad ratio may mean that the owner has decided to take money out of the business. Check the ratio for previous years. Has it got better or worse? Has the owner been letting the business build up, or bleeding it of any 'spare' cash? Two useful credit ratios may show you what is happening.

Credit ratios

The two ratios are:

creditors: purchases

and:

debts: credit sales

What are these telling us? The point behind them is usually made clearer by converting the figures produced by applying the ratios to the accounts into figures showing how many days the average debt or credit is outstanding.

Say that the creditors' figure is £5,000 and the total purchases are £50,000. That gives a rather meaningless ratio of 1:10. Now, multiply the first figure by 365 (or 52 if you want weeks), and then divide it by the second figure. That gives a figure of 36 days or 5 weeks. This means the business is taking 5 weeks on average to pay its bills. If creditors are usually extending 30 days net terms, that is not so bad. If their terms are 14 or 7 days (which you also need to find out), then things do not look too good.

Take the debts ratio. Say the figures are £20,000 on total sales of £75,000, or 1:3.75. On a daily basis, this is about 97 days or 14 weeks. Something may be badly wrong here. Whether or not it is bad will depend on the business. What would spell bankruptcy for a greengrocer would be a miracle in selling an aircraft. But it may be that not all the customers are that slow in paying – rather, the figure hides some bad debts that are unlikely to be paid.

Here again, trends are useful. How have these two ratios changed from one year to another? If they are very healthy, there may be scope for changing them in your favour by speeding up the collection of the debts and slowing down the rate of paying creditors. A colleague of mine took an extra million pounds in for his business in one year just by doing that, and did not really affect the business's relationships to its customers or suppliers. But it can be worked the other way, if your suppliers suddenly tighten up on their terms, and you are relying too heavily on their credit.

Business efficiency

Other standard tests applied to businesses are those showing its **gross profit ratio** and **net profit ratio**. These are obtained by turning the ratio of gross profits, and net profits to total sales, into percentages. The percentages do not mean very much on their own. Again, trends are all important. Is the business becoming more or less profitable? If so, why? Have a look at individual overheads in the same way. In many businesses the rates have been rising very fast in recent years. Have profits kept pace? How do the figures compare with the usual profit ratios for that kind of business, or the national averages?

Shelf life and shelf rent

If your business is selling goods, particularly retail sales, other figures can help here in showing the real throughput of stock in the business. There are two measures to look for, again from the accounts. The first is the figure for sales per square metre of the shop or store. For this you compare the sales figures for a given period with the area of the showroom or shop. Another figure is the 'shelf life' of the stock. This can be judged by finding out how many times the stock is turned over in a year. Compare the opening and closing balances of stock with the total throughput of stock during the year.

For example, the figures may show that the stock is on average turned over ten times a year. Whether that is good or bad will very much depend on the type of business, and also whether the business is carrying a relatively high or relatively low level of stock. Read that with the rental costs, and we get some idea of 'shelf rent', the amount it costs us to store stock between purchase and sale. If our stock is turning over ten times a year, it is costing about ten per cent of the annual rent, rates, etc, to store the stock between purchase and sale.

In most retail businesses, a decent level of stock must be carried to attract the customer. But in a manufacturing or service business, it may be possible to reduce the stock levels almost to zero. As we discuss below (in Chapter 6, 'Plan it'), adopting the 'just in time' approach to stock buying may mean we have no stock rent to pay at all. Lax stock control may be tying up large amounts of cash.

Return on capital

A final figure to watch for is the return on owner's capital. Find the ratio:

net profits: owner's capital

and you really find out whether your money might not be better left in a deposit account! Going back to our cut flower business for example, if we put in, say, £30,000 to buy the business and stock, and the net profit is £12,000, the return is 40%. Not so bad, except that if we put the money in the bank we would make perhaps £3,000 or more anyway, leaving £10,000 to pay us for our efforts. How much effort is it? Was the ad right in saying it was easily run?

Making comparisons

Armed with these figures, we have some idea of the real shape of the business. Better still, we should compare it with similar businesses. This is how the taxmen check on who is and who is not fiddling their accounts. They work out the gross and net profits (and other ratios) for all the businesses of a particular kind in an area. It is a fair bet that if they find that the gross profit of nearly all the local fish and chip shops is, say, 35%, then the owner who claims only to be making a profit of 15% in a shop that clearly is doing a fair trade, is on the fiddle.

Usefully to you, the Revenue publish these figures as their *Business Economic Notes* on a national basis. The Government's *Business Monitors* for each sector of industry also give a national picture of the profitability of a business, and other information may be available through local libraries. Beyond that, you are going to need to consult appropriate experts who can advise you about the business from their own local experience.

What changes can you make?

We now know from the figures what the business has really been like. Next we must see what scope there is for improvement from our own efforts. The accounts should already have given several clues about the speed of turnover of stock, of payment of bills and collection of debts, the stock levels of the business, the cost of stock storage and the profit ratios, and any exploitable reserves. They may show room for a quick improvement in reducing stock levels, speeding up collection of credit or in other ways. Is there room also for expanding the turnover or increasing the profit margins?

This part is not so easy to judge – though don't forget the ten year test we looked at in the last Chapter may help. What do we know of changes in the locality, and what can we find out? Are there more or fewer potential customers in the area or business five or ten years from now?

Try and get the 'feel' of the business. If you are buying a retail business or a service trade relying on passing trade, walk or drive round the area and find out what the competition is. Check all the points we examine in 'Go where'. Having done that, if you are going ahead, bring in the experts, and get planning. Buying an existing business is not an excuse for avoiding either of these.

The price is never right

Only after careful planning, and listening to your experts, are you really in a position to decide to buy. The crucial question now is the price. You can get an agent or your solicitor or accountant to deal with this, but they can only advise on the crucial question of what is your maximum price. This depends on what the business is really worth to you. Work out this maximum and stick to it. Even if you do not employ a negotiator, you will almost certainly be dealing with a professional acting for the seller. Don't be too readily persuaded by his tactics.

To value the business, take each part of it separately. What are the premises worth? If you are buying a freehold, a valuer can give you a good comparative figure fairly readily. For leases, it depends on the security of tenure, rent level, the condition of the premises, service charges or other obligations in addition to the rent, and the location and nature of the property. The price for fixtures and fittings should take into account what replacements and improvements you will need for out of date machinery. Examine the trading stock to see how much of it is saleable only at reduced prices. What is the goodwill and knowhow worth? Possibly very little, but in practice this covers the difference between what the assets of the business are worth and what you have to pay. Is the difference justified?

Armed with this information, set your initial price. Do not take too much notice at this stage of the seller's asking price. The agent will almost certainly have left room for manoeuvre if after a quick sale. It is also likely that the price will be more than the business is worth to allow the seller to recover the agent's commission. Beyond that, your guides must be the maximum amount the business is worth and, of course, the amount you can sensibly afford.

Joining a franchise

At its best, buying into a franchise is buying a share of someone else's success, so that it becomes your success also. For this reason, many are attracted to the idea of setting up their new business as part of a national franchise. Success stories such as Kentucky Fried Chicken and the BSM Driving Schools make this look an attractive idea, whilst the prevalence of an operation such as Spar grocers shows how common the approach is in practice.

The central approach of franchising is simple. In exchange for a franchise fee and continuing royalties, the franchisee buys the right to sell the franchisor's products or services backed by the franchisor's own research, knowhow and marketing. The point is that the product or service, being advertised nationally, or even world-wide, will command a very good price from customers. This gives the seller a good profit margin, to be shared with the franchisor.

Unfortunately, there are some very bad buys in the franchising market, as well as very good buys, and a great range in between. As ever, be on your guard, and investigate a proposed franchisor's proposal with great care before signing into the franchise.

What does it cost?

The price of a franchise will reflect what you get. The franchise fee can be anything from £5,000 to £350,000. In addition, you will need the other start-up costs of a business: premises, equipment, fees, initial stock (see Chapter 11, 'Raising cash'). Thereafter, you buy stock through the franchisor, so will pay their price for replacement stock. That cost is beyond your control, and can be above market costs. You may also be required to pay a royalty based on the value of sales. That creates a gap between your gross profit and net profit from the business which will have to be paid regularly.

What you get in return will be set out in an extremely important document, the **franchise contract**. You get the right to sell franchised goods or services, using the franchisor's name and goodwill, trade marks and knowhow. You should also get the franchisor's help in setting up your franchise operation. This covers help in finding, acquiring and fitting out the premises, assistance in arranging the necessary finance, and training for you and for your staff, plus advertising support for your new business.

Your contract will be for a fixed period, probably between five and ten years. During the period of the franchise you should receive the continuing support of the franchisor both by way of advertising and as advice to you, plus the continuing supply of stock. At the same time, the franchisor will supervise your business, making sure your quality control and business standards meet those required in the contract.

This inspection is also part of the franchise contract. You will be required under that contract to sell your goods or services strictly in accordance with the franchisor's product image. This may cover opening hours, uniforms, even – it would seem in some places – the words you use to customers. The franchisor must protect the product presented by each franchisee for the benefit of itself and all other franchisees.

Are franchises a good idea?

The best ones certainly are, but they are also the expensive ones. The following points will indicate whether a franchise is good for you:

- A franchise is **your own business** – but subject to tight restrictions under most franchise contracts. Will you be happy with these?
- **The product should be well tested** or established in the market and the franchisor should be committed to keeping it that way. But if the franchisor disappears or fails, where does that leave you?
- The **stock** will be branded and subject to quality control – but it will be at the franchisor's price and subject to its conditions. If you find better elsewhere, you will not be able to buy it. If the franchisor does, and buys it, you benefit.
- The franchisor will provide you with **training and advice** based on much wider experience of the industry than you have – or is it? And how much advice and training do you get?
- Franchises cost money, but should produce the **profits** to pay for it. Does the franchise let you earn those profits before the franchisor gets its share, or is the fee demanded first? If you are paying up front, is there any real

incentive for the franchisor to bother about you once you have paid?

- What happens at **the end of the contract** or if you want out? However successful you are, the business is not all yours to sell. Does that matter in the long term, or are your objectives confined to the period of the franchise contract?

Don't be ripped off

The worst forms of franchise are so misleading that they are illegal: **pyramid selling** and the like. Yet thousands still get taken in by them, and hand their life savings to a con-man in the certainty that there is a fortune to be made. There is – from them, not by them.

Watch out for anything resembling a pyramid selling operation. They are like those chain-letters that still do the rounds. Send the card to the first person on the list, then four cards to friends. In a few weeks you will receive hundreds of cards from all over the world. I, for one, have several times dutifully sent off my cards. I have never once received one in reply. That is the fate of the pyramid seller, too.

Pyramid selling looks more sophisticated than the chain cards trick. You will buy the 'exclusive' right to become a middle man in some sales operation – for example, growing some magic culture to cure the world's ills. You pay a premium for the culture, but once you have grown some, you have the right to sell it to others for a premium, as do they, and so on. It is a fair bet that the franchise fee will be all up-front, simply because the franchisor will not stay around long enough for you to discover either that the culture will not grow, or that no one else will buy it from you, or both.

Between the rip-off, and the highly respectable and established operations such as Budget Car Hire or the national fast food outlets, there is no clear line. So you need advice from independent advisors – not the franchisor. Make sure you get a solicitor to look at the franchise contract for you. Get the franchisor's own accounts and the projected cash figures for your proposed franchise, and get an accountant to look at them. Your bank may well have a specialist franchise manager who will help (and may have inside knowledge about existing outlets of the franchise). Finally, get in touch with the franchisors' trade association, the **British Franchise Association** (address at the end of this book). It has useful literature, and can offer advice. Its members follow a set code of practice, so check if your proposed franchisor is a member, and if not, why not.

Either way, you should do the same planning of your business as if you were starting from scratch, as we discuss in Chapter 6, 'Plan it' below, and you should seek expert advice in just the same way (see Chapter 4, 'Get the experts in').

4 Get the experts in

Most small businessmen and women are do-it-yourself experts. I do not mean that they are very good at mending the secretaries' kettle, repainting the office or repairing the delivery van. No doubt they can do all these, but they probably have better things to do with their time. Rather, they have to be their own buyers, salesmen, public relations advisors, production engineers, personnel officers, safety officers . . . the list seems endless. Not for them the luxury of the large corporation, which can hire an expert team to handle every facet of the business.

The danger, as with all DIY, is that self-sufficiency gets carried too far. Just as in writing this book I have relied on the advice of experts in several fields, so should you in getting your business going. Even if you want to, in practice you will not be able to get far without the assistance of at least an accountant, a solicitor, a bank and an insurance expert – and you would be foolish to try. So act positive, and get them on your side from the start.

Do not assume it will cost you a fortune. Advice from several of the sources below is free – some may even give *you* money. Those that do charge will often save you more money than they cost you, provided you know what you want from them. Nonetheless the charge rates of expert professionals are often £150 an hour or more, so wasting their time is wasting your money. It also pays to get estimates of costs from accountants and solicitors.

Who can help, and how?

Local enterprise agencies

These invaluable (to the community) and free (to the small businessman) bodies have sprung up all over Britain in the last few years. Their strength is that they are local bodies set up to meet local needs. As a result, they have no one way of working. Nor do they have any set form of name, though they are usually named after their localities. They do have the same objective – to offer advice and help to those wanting to set up on their own in that area. They are funded by donations from councils, local businesses and charities, and have staff seconded to them by major businesses so can provide their services free to the new business.

If you cannot easily find the name of your local enterprise agency, contact **Business in the Community** (address at the end of this book), the national body coordinating LEAs (for short), or the Small Firms Service (see below).

An LEA can offer initial help on any aspect of your business which you can think of, and then those you haven't thought about. It is staffed by people with direct experience, and has a wide circle of contacts on which it can draw, ranging from grant-making bodies to local councils and, because it is a mixture of both public sector and private sector, the local professions, banks and others whose help you need. Its staff will counsel you on what you ought, and ought not, be doing, and, if felt necessary, warn you off what they feel to be bad ideas. For the great majority the enterprise agency will offer encouragement and support. Either way, seek their help at an early stage.

LEAs also often run courses on aspects of running your own business, both for those just thinking of starting and for those who have got going. They continue to help as the business develops – though, as one manager put it, they don't so often get people coming back. Those who are succeeding tend to assume they don't need any further help.

Those who are failing tend to assume they will just be made to feel foolish. Neither is true. Both still need help, and will get it.

Small Firms Service

SFS is part of the Department of Employment. It has ten offices in England. In Scotland and Wales, it is run by the Scottish Development Agency or Welsh Development Agency respectively. The offices may seem remote, but they are only as far away as your telephone. Ask the operator for **Freefone Enterprise** and you will be put in touch with your nearest office free of charge.

SFS sells itself as a 'big help to a small business'. Its purpose is to help both the new and the established small business. It does this through four separate but related areas of activity. It offers both an **enquiry service** and a **signposting service**. Both of these are free of charge, and are backed by computer based data systems. Linked with that, the SFS produces free booklets. This is supported by the Department of Trade and Industry, which produces a free bimonthly newspaper, *In Business Now*.

SFS can also provide a **counsellor**, or business advisor to help with any problem. The time of counsellors is free for the first three sessions, but after that the counsellor has to be paid for by the business he or she is advising. The DTI (the Department for Enterprise as it calls itself) helps this with the **Enterprise Initiative**, giving aid to small business by private sector counsellors working with Government financial support and training. Substantial funds are available to subsidise individual businesses seeking counselling help and further training. To find out about these contact the **DTI** (addresses at the end of this book) or use their freefone number (see end).

The fourth aspect of the SFS service is its **Business Development Service** aimed at established small firms seeking guidance on expansion plans. Again, initial guidance is free, but after that has to be paid for by the business. This is also supplemented by the DTI Enterprise Initiative.

Go by training

The **MSC** (Manpower Services Commission) has several important roles in helping the small business. In particular, it is responsible for financing and encouraging the running of training courses such as self-employment programmes and small business programmes. There are now a very large number of courses for the small business, and especially for the new business, all over the country. Start-up courses for the new business are often available free, and all are available at subsidised prices. Contact the MSC (addresses at the end of this book) to get a full list of the courses now available in your area, or contact your nearest college, polytechnic or university to find out what they are running. The **Open University** runs distance-learning courses for those starting or running small businesses. By all accounts, British managers and small business owners are still far less well trained than their competitors. Will that apply to you?

Training help is also provided by **Industry Training Boards**. These are aimed at providing training courses to help businesses get better at their own skills. There are a whole series of boards some of which have help specifically for the self-employed. They will also be able to offer counselling and individual advice, and sometimes financial help. Get further details from the MSC (address at end).

Other Government help

Another Government-funded body that may help is **CoSIRA**, the Council for Small Industries in Rural Areas. CoSIRA is specifically given the job of getting small industries going in country areas, and keeping them going. It has funds to make direct grants for this, and can also help obtain grants and loans from elsewhere. In Scotland, the same job is done by the Highlands and Islands Board (HIB) and the Scottish Development Agency (SDA), and in Wales by the Welsh Development Agency (WDA).

Local councils

Some local councils provide a great deal of help – including financial help – to small businesses in their areas. These councils have special units (often called **Economic Development Units**) for the job, and are able to help not just with dealing with other departments of the council (such as the planners) but other local contacts as well. Other councils content themselves with advertising the joys of working in their area, with no direct backup (though they may give financial support to the local enterprise agency to do that instead). Others just rest on their laurels, and are content for you to rest on yours. That's one reason why Chapter 7, 'Go where?' in this book is important.

Help with information

One much neglected free local service you should make a point of using is your **local library** service. If you are one of those who assumes that a library is merely a place to borrow tatty novels you are missing valuable help. Libraries might be better called **information centres** (as a few are) because they provide access to a tremendous amount of useful information, as we see in Chapter 8, 'What are you selling?'

If your local library is small, it is part of a chain linked to the county (or city) commercial or **business library**. The London Business Library or Manchester Commercial Library, for example, are superb collections of reference books and journals spanning the world. Library staff will suggest where you can find the details about your own query. More generally, you will find books such as this one and more specialist volumes on the open shelves – usually under **classification number 658**. (If that's where you got this from in the first place, find out about the rest of the library's facilities when you take it back.)

Special help for the young

Government help, such as the **Enterprise Allowance** scheme, is aimed primarily at those aged at least 18, the assumption being that the Youth Training Scheme is the best avenue for those who leave full time education before that. Careers Office help will be available for those wanting to aim at their own business from the start.

One private scheme which is open to those aged from 16 is **Livewire**. This is a competition in form, for developing the best business ideas. Although some get the prizes, everyone can gain because counselling and advice is available to all participants throughout the period of the competition.

Other initiatives offering advice and support are **Head Start** and **Instant Muscle**. Head Start is aimed at those aged between 17 and 25 and its main support is through part-time training and helping with your business plan plus help from a counsellor for a year. Instant Muscle is aimed at getting help to the young in deprived city areas. In Wales, the Young Initiative Programme, run by the Welsh Development Agency, aims straight at those in and leaving school. Its sessions start in schools and can be followed by further sessions with business counsellors for those interested in going into their own businesses (for addresses see the end of the book).

The Prince's Youth Business Trust

We introduced this important initiative for those aged 18 to 25 in the Foreword. It provides finance, professional advice, training and education to assist young people of limited means, in setting up or developing their own small businesses, either as sole traders or in partnership with others. It carries out this work through its own national network and in co-operation with other job creation organisations and enterprise agencies.

More recently the Trust has expanded its age limit for financial support for young disabled people up to and including the age of 30.

The Trust is particularly concerned with helping young people who are disadvantaged, whether for social, economic, environmental or physical reasons. They must have viable, imaginative business propositions plus plenty of enthusiasm and determination to succeed.

By February 1990 the Trust had advised over 20,000 young people and provided financial help and tutorial support to over 9,000 of the most deserving of them.

How does it work?

Young people usually hear of the Trust through Job Centres, Enterprise Agencies, Youth Organisations, other charitable bodies and, of course, by word of mouth.

All applications for assistance (whether financial or not) must be supported by a business plan. Every applicant will receive help from one of the Trust's own Regional Co-ordinators or an advisor recognised by the Trust, (for example, from a Youth Enterprise Centre). Once the proposals are finalised, most are presented for assessment to one of 36 regional boards. In most instances the applicants may be asked to put their case personally.

In order to qualify for financial assistance the plan must be considered to have a reasonable chance of success.

What support does it provide?

- *Grants* in the form of bursaries of up to £1,500 per person or £3,000 per business. These are available to applicants of limited means who are unemployed or disadvantaged, and will be made to help them meet the setting up costs of their new business.
  Increasingly, the provision of a loan to enable the business to expand, will follow the initial grant – 'adding value' to the original support for the business.
- *Low interest loans* of up to £5,000 these can be paid out as a lump sum with the repayment terms incorporating advantageous interest rates.
- *Advice and support* for all successful applicants, provided on an ongoing basis by Business Advisors. They maintain regular contact with the businesses, monitoring progress and offering advice in problem solving. In addition, training in business management and basic accounting can be provided.
- *Test Marketing grants* of up to £250 for proving that a market for a product/service exists. **Training grants** for supported businesses can also be obtained.
- *Work experience* and **business training models** have been developed by the Trust specifically in London, West Midlands and West Yorkshire with the substantial help of the Employment Department. The Trust's training requirements in these areas have been handed over to

Task Undertakings which is developing its training operations nationally. Its Patron is the Prince of Wales. The Prince's Youth Business Trust is very keen to ensure that all applicants have received adequate training to prepare themselves for self employment and it counsels and advises applicants about the most appropriate training they need to undertake.

How is it organised?

The Headquarters of the Trust is in London, where a small staff deal with central services.

Responsibility for all day-to-day activities is devolved to local communities through Regional Boards. There are currently 36 Regional Boards throughout the United Kingdom. All Regional Boards are chaired by a local voluntary leader who has a particular concern for the young and the unemployed. Each Regional Board is supported by at least one full time professional **Regional Co-ordinator** seconded from industry. This Co-ordinator is responsible for the day-to-day running of the Trust in that region.

Throughout the country the Trust is supported by over 3,000 **Business Advisers** working on a voluntary, part-time basis. They provide training in basic management, accounts and more specific skills. At least one Advisor is assigned to most PYBT supported businesses and are often drawn from other organisations, including Local Enterprise Agencies with which the Trust co-operates.

Other help

For minority communities – Whilst none of the agencies so far described discriminates in any way, sadly the community often does. To help those minorities caught by this, **Project**

Fullemploy has as one of its aims helping those aged between 18–30 from minority ethnic origins to get started in self-employment (address at end). Some local authorities will also give special help to the minority groups.

For the disabled – Special help and advice is available through Jobcentres from the Government's **Disablement Advisory Service** and **Disablement Resettlement Officers** for those who find their work impaired, or difficult, because of a disability. Help is also available through many of the agencies noted above. A private organisation which can also offer help is the **Disabled Living Foundation** (address at end).

In special areas – See Chapter 7, 'Go Where?' below.

In particular industries – Contact the Industry Training Board, if there is one. Help may also be forthcoming through the **trade association** relevant to your business – get the address through your local library. One industry given particular support is tourism (also one of the UK's fastest growing industries). Financial support, advice and support are available through the national **Tourist Boards** (addresses at end). Your local enterprise agency or the Small Firms Service will also be able to tell you about other help specific to your kind of business, including special MSC and other courses, and grant schemes.

Protecting your ideas

If your new business venture is founded on an original idea of your own then you will want to protect this idea in such a way as to be able to be the sole supplier of those goods or services. The most secure means of doing this is to patent your invention with the Patent Office in High Holborn, but be warned this is a lengthy procedure and can cost several hundreds of pounds. As well as patenting an invention you may wish to register a particular Trade Mark or Service

Mark so that it can be unique to your business. There is also a means of protecting industrial designs. All these possibilities are explained in publications available from the Patent Office but when you read them you may feel that it is advisable to get professional help from a patent agent. A list of names is available from the Chartered Institute of Patent Agents in High Holborn. (Tel: 01-405 4950).

Copyright

If your business is to rely upon original works of art or craft then there is also a way of protecting these, this is what's known as 'copyright'. By copyrighting drawings, books, recordings etc you will be able to control the reproduction of these works and avoid any unauthorised plagiarism. You do not have to register a copyright but you must make sure that your original work has the international copyright symbol displayed (this is the letter C inside a circle) and is signed and dated. Copyright lasts for 50 years after the death of the originator.

Appointing your own experts

The wealth of help and assistance that can be gained by anyone setting up in business is considerable, but your need for expert assistance does not stop there. You will, in addition, and from the beginning, need the services of your own professionals. In particular you will need an accountant, a bank, a lawyer, and insurance advice.

All these services now compete strongly for the favour of the small business owner, and offer a far wider range of services than they traditionally used to – with competition in some fields between all of them. But there are still things each can do that the other professions cannot, and you need to form your own team of experts. Do that right at the beginning with all of them. Do not leave appointing your lawyer or accountant until you hit a problem. They will probably discover that you have hit several others you did not know about, as well.

Accountants

Anyone can call herself or himself an accountant. The only qualification for having the word in a letterhead is having the money to pay for printing it! Protect yourself by appointing someone who is a member of the major accounting institutions. They impose high standards on all entrants, impose codes of conduct and have professional insurance schemes to protect you against losing money through an accountant's professional errors. And talk to a number of accountants about what you want and what they have to offer.

It is said, only half in fun, that to choose an accountant, go into the office with your books and ask the accountant to find what your profits are. Don't appoint the fellow who promptly sits down with his calculator and works it out for you – appoint instead the one who says 'What figure do you want?' More seriously, you need someone to help you run the finances of the business, to sort out tax questions, to make sure your books are keeping a true record of your business, to check the validity of your accounts each year, and probably check on the financial viability of your plans.

Strictly, you are only required by law to appoint an accountant if your business is run through a company. If so, you need an auditor for your company accounts, and this is a major job of accountants. Unless you really know what you are doing, you should also appoint one if you are a sole trader, and certainly if you are in a partnership.

Accounting firms vary enormously in size and coverage. The very largest are huge businesses with branches in every major city in the world, and specialising not only in accounting and auditing but equally in taxation, management consultancy, personnel selection, technical training, aspects of legal compliance, business formation, development financing, import and export work, payroll and pension problems, and so on . . . far removed from the one-person band, able to offer a much more limited service, but doing it personally and locally.

CA, ACCA, CIMA

Check that the accountant belongs to an appropriate professional association. The main ones are: **CA** or **FCA** – the Institutes of Chartered Accountants (there are separate English, Scottish and Irish institutes). Chartered accountants must undergo rigorous training plus a three year training period before qualifying. Most are graduates. The other major body is the Chartered Association of Certified Accountants (**FCCA** or **ACCA**). There is a more specialist body whose members may be of assistance, **CIMA**, the Institute of Management Accountants.

How do you choose your accountants? The best way to start is by seeking personal recommendations. Ask others with similar problems whom they would get to do the work, and why. Another point to watch: your interests may be best served by a smaller firm, where you are not just another client, but where there is someone qualified to look after you whilst your usual accountant is ill or on holiday; or it may be in a larger firm which has specialist skills and contacts in your area of business, for example a local office in a country to which you intend to export.

Management accounts

If you are thinking of buying someone else's business, an accountant is trained in the mumbo-jumbo and hidden problems in a set of business accounts, and you should get him to read the accounts. This is management accounting, that is, the use of the figures to analyse the strengths and weaknesses of a business to plan ahead, so that the business can be developed in ways that exploit those strengths and eliminate the weaknesses. While the ordinary accounts tell you whether you made a profit or a loss, management accounts should show which parts of your business made the most profits, and how much, the effects of changes in your business, and where your overheads seem too high.

Finally, fees. There is no fixed basis for accountancy fees, though firms usually base them on time spent and the hourly charge rate of the person devoting time to your work. Each visit, letter and telephone call is charged at the rate appropriate to a partner or trainee, as the case may be. But you can still ask for estimates or even tenders, as competition is strong.

Lawyers

Your legal advisers are best chosen before you suddenly need them for some legal action. As with accountants, there are a few jobs for which in practical terms employing a lawyer is unavoidable, but a great many other services that a commercially-minded solicitor can offer. Look at the amount of law in other chapters of this book: hiring and sacking staff; getting permission for your business; getting your contract terms right; making sure your business structure is right . . . as well as court cases and property transfers.

Unlike accountancy, the law is a closed profession. No one

can call themselves a **solicitor** unless they have passed the
Law Society's examinations and served a training contract,
plus, before they set up on their own, three further years
working as an assistant to another solicitor. All solicitors
acting for the public must have a practising certificate which
must be renewed yearly, must comply with strict financial
regulations and a code of ethics, and must be insured against
causing their clients losses. **Barristers**, who handle court work
and give specialist advice on the law, can only be instructed
by a solicitor or other professional, so cannot be approached
directly by a businessman.

Law firms tend to specialise or, in the bigger firms, have
specialist departments. Solicitors are now allowed to
advertise, and should tell you what services they cover. Many
bigger firms have brochures describing who they are and
what they do. The Law Society has set up a scheme called
'Lawyers for Enterprise' designed to help solicitors help
small businesses, and many solicitors' firms belong to this
scheme which is advertised by a pair of scissors cutting
through red tape. Ask at your local library or local law society
for a list of those involved in the scheme in your area. The
points about size and cost made about accountants apply
equally here.

Appoint your lawyers early. For example, if buying into a
franchise, get their advice on the franchise contract. If setting
up a partnership, get advice about it at the beginning. If
getting new premises, you will need a solicitor to do the
conveyancing, and should certainly get him to read and advise
on the terms of any lease you are asked to sign. It is standard
lawyer's advice never to sign anything you have not read. But
have you ever tried reading a ninety-page lease? Don't. Get
them to look at it for you. Further, a good lawyer's many
contacts, as those of a good accountant, may prove very
useful to your business in wider ways.

Banks

Banks have been developing very rapidly in recent years in help for small businesses. Indeed, it is almost too easy for some to get money out of them (see Chapter 11, 'Raising cash'). On the other hand, someone once defined a banker as a person who would lend you his umbrella when the sun was shining, but demand it back the moment it starts raining. He's still right. Perhaps the difference now is that they are more prepared to endure the summer showers before recalling the umbrella.

The big banks have recently completely revised their approach to smaller customers, and they will now offer you attractive literature and some very helpful advice. More important, they have **small business advice units** staffed by experts to help with your financial plans and financial control of your business, and will help set up not just loans but mortgages and insurance as well.

Even if you do not want the bank's wider services you will still need a good banker – unless you believe that money, not springs, makes the best stuffing for a mattress. However small and simple your business, you need reliable bank accounts through which cheques and credit transfers can be cleared and honoured with speed and without query. This is always better done through separate accounts to your personal accounts, so you keep a check on the business funds. If you are handling your customers' money in any large amount, separate accounts may be wise, linked with deposit accounts so the money does not lie idle.

Like it or not, your bank manager will soon learn a lot about you and your finances. It helps to let them know what you are doing, and get the advice they can offer. You will find that your manager is usually willing to talk generally when you first meet, and probably has some useful tips about local business. But remember also that, unlike the accountant or lawyer who is employed by you and for you, the bank remains an independent concern which is selling you its products.

Insurance advisers

At an early stage you will have to start thinking about insurance. If you are buying premises, using your own transport, or buying tools you will have to make sure that you are fully insured against the inevitable list of potential disasters that can befall you such as fire, theft and so on.

You are also going to have to start thinking about insuring yourself and that doesn't just mean life assurance. Planning for a pension is a way of making sure that your future is taken care of (with some attractive tax benefits thrown in for good measure). Personal health insurance can be a valuable form of protection when your entire income depends on your ability to work. Finally, life assurance, which is the only way of guaranteeing that your family will be protected if the unthinkable happens. If you have a need to borrow money, then your bank will almost certainly need some form of life cover as security – security for them that is, not you.

Advice on insurance matters can come from a number of sources but they all have to be officially authorised if they are advising you on investment matters (which includes life assurance and pensions). These rules rather restrict the help that your solicitor or accountant can give you – they can advise you in general terms that, for example, life assurance might be a good idea but they can't go into much detail on the precise type of life insurance that might best suit you.

After that, you will need either to talk to an authorised insurance **broker** (who will be acting on behalf of several companies) or to a **company representative** (who will be authorised to act on behalf of one company). The choice is really down to you – ideally, you should find someone who you can get on with and who will take the time and trouble to find out about you and your business.

The quartet of accountant, lawyer, banker and insurance adviser should constitute your back-up team of professional advisers, though, as we discuss in several places, you will probably need other professionals to help from time to time.

5 Two's a company?

At an early stage in setting up your business you must decide what structure the business will have. If you go it alone you will be a **sole proprietor**. If there are two or more of you, you can form a **partnership** or **cooperative**, or one of you can employ the others, or you keep your interests separated. Alternatively, you can turn the business into a **company** so that the business belongs to the company not you, although you may be the managing director.

Watch two key points. First, are there – or should there be – two or more people involved together in the business? The other person could be your wife or husband, a good friend, someone lending you money, or a former work colleague. Whoever it is, you would both need to sort out your working relationships fully. Second, don't rush off and turn the business into a company without thinking why. It could be a costly mistake.

The sole trader

It is one of our less trumpeted liberties that we may set up our own businesses, and stand or fall by our own abilities without a state licence to do so. Consumer protection measures and other laws mean it is not quite as simple as that these days, but it is the Government's avowed aim to keep red tape to a minimum. The Government makes a standing request of you. If you have suggestions for deregulation, send them to the **Enterprise and Deregulation Unit** (address at end).

When you set up, check if you need any permission to carry on that business at that place (see Chapter 7, 'Go where?'). In an increasing number of businesses you also need either a qualification or a licence. For example, although anyone can call themselves an accountant, not everyone can give insurance or legal advice, nor can they call themselves a bank.

One problem is that local rules often vary. You may need local permission to open a coffee shop as well as an off-licence. The need for taxi licences is well known, but less so is the need for licences for nursing homes – though local councils deal with both. Tobacconists need a licence, whilst newspapers should be registered with the Post Office . . ., and so the list goes on. There are hundreds of different licensing requirements, many run by local councils. Check with your local council or your professional advisors to see what requirements there are affecting your business. There will almost certainly be some, if only your duty to tell the tax authorities (see Chapter 14, 'Your share – their share').

Choosing the business name

One requirement must be watched by everyone going into business – the right name. You can conduct business under your own name (perhaps with the suffix '& Co' added – that makes no legal difference). But you may decide on another name. If you use any name other than your own surname, perhaps together with your own forename or initials, you must comply with the **Business Names Act**. This requires you to put your own name, and your address, on all business letters, written orders for goods or services, invoices and receipts and written demands for payment of business debts. Failure to do so is an offence for which people can be fined.

Don't pinch someone else's name. They can object to your name if they can show you are **passing-off** your business as theirs. If your business name is the same as or too similar to that of another business, with the result that their customers might confuse the two businesses, court action could be taken against you to prevent you using that name and also to get damages from you.

Logos (like the VW sign on cars) are protected **trade marks**, and pictures, music, special phrases ('It's finger-lickin' good') are protected **copyright**, and belong to their owners just as much as other kinds of property, so you should not use them for your business without permission. That is one of the key aspects of a franchise agreement. And remember, if you get a good logo, name, phrase or design you can protect it too, though you should seek legal advice about it.

In business together

Married (and other) couples – We have already seen that if one of a couple goes into business, it should be with the other's support. In practice the other will inevitably be involved in some way. Does that mean both should be partners in the business, or one should employ the other? It may mean that one of the couple does the work whilst the other puts up the money. At the other extreme, it may mean that the partner going into business thinks it wise to transfer his interest in the family home and other property to the other partner. Though, as to the latter idea, one divorcee ruefully remarked to me that it was swapping a bad risk for a worse one! For myself, I don't agree, but there are some serious issues to be thought about.

If the couple both work at a business without reaching an agreement, custom often regards the business as the husband's. The law would not agree – for tax, social security, family law and other purposes the business will normally be jointly that of husband and wife, and profits should be shared equally. If the couple want it some other way, they should agree otherwise. Certainly, if the wife is playing a small part in the business, it may be better that she is an employee (see Chapter 15, 'Being the boss').

The business may also put the family home on the line. If a lender wants it as security for, say, the husband's loan, the wife will usually be asked to agree. This is because even where the husband is sole owner of the house, the wife has rights to live there. These rights take priority over those of a mortgagee. If the husband defaults on his loan, and the wife has not agreed to the loan because, for example, she had never heard of it, the mortgagee cannot sell the house.

Others working together – There are several ways that people can go into business together. One can agree to put up the money whilst another does the work. The one putting up the money need not be involved in the other's business, and can just be an investor. Often, such lenders want a say in how the business runs. In that case, lender and borrower must get together either through a partnership (where the lender will be a 'sleeping partner', see below) or a company, where the lender will be a shareholder and, probably, director.

In other cases, two or more people will work side by side in the same business. There is a lot to be gained by arranging to work together with others in a team helping each other. If all have a share in the business, they have to become a partnership or a cooperative or jointly form a company in which all have a stake. By some route they must determine who runs the business, and what share each has in it. If there is no agreement but the team goes ahead anyway, the law will treat the team as being equal partners.

Partnerships

A business partnership may come into existence like an arranged marriage, with proper attention to formality and detail. Or it may happen like a love affair, so that it is only when the euphoria has worn off, and problems become apparent, that you realise what has happened.

The law requires no formalities of a business partnership. Partners may have introduced a lot of money into the business, or none at all. A partnership exists, to quote the law, whenever two or more persons 'carry on business in common with a view of profit'. If people jointly run a business, sharing business decisions, sharing profits and the risk of losses, and working together, they will be partners. The law imposes on them rights and duties as partners to each other unless and until they agree otherwise. Whatever they agree, one or more of the partners must be personally liable for all partnership debts. If the business fails, the partners will lose out completely.

Agreement is most important. Although the law lays down rules (in the Partnership Acts) governing partnership rules, all these rules can be changed by agreement. That is why partners should always draw up an agreement with proper advice. Do not assume, because you are good friends before the partnership, that you will make good business colleagues, or even stay friends.

Partners' rights and duties

By law, partners are equally entitled to share in profits and are equally at risk for the losses. What is more, each partner is responsible for the full debts of the partnership, so a creditor can sue any of them. Each partner also has full authority to act as agent for all other partners, and to pledge the credit of all partners for the business. What is more, a former partner may remain responsible for partnership debts after he has left. The tax position will depend on the separate earnings of the partners, as well as their joint earnings.

Partners can leave the partnership, and withdraw their capital at will without notice, unless otherwise agreed. No provision is made for a partner who has an accident or reaches retirement age. Decisions on matters such as this have to be joint decisions, and in many cases each partner has an effective right of veto.

It is quite common to have a partnership where some of those involved are **sleeping partners**. These are partners whose money is involved in the business, and who may have some decision making powers, but who are not concerned with the management and day-to-day running of the business. Their money is in the business as an investment. It is also possible to have **limited partnerships**, where some partners are sleeping partners whose capital is at risk but who, under the partnership terms, are liable to lose only that capital, and do not have unlimited liability. In either case at least one partner must be a **general partner** with unlimited liability for debts. Normally, where such kinds of arrangements are wanted, companies have provided an easier way of doing it.

A final point. When someone leaves a partnership, all the customers and suppliers have to be notified. Otherwise the former partner may still be liable for partnership debts, and the new partners for his debts. Also, a badly timed breakup of a partnership may significantly increase the tax payable by the partners. For both reasons, it is worth getting proper advice at the end of a partnership as well as at the beginning.

Checklist: Partnership agreements

It will pay to get your agreement drawn up properly by a solicitor in all but the simplest case. Here are some things the agreement should cover:

- When does the partnership start?
  Where is it to be carried on?
  What is the business of the partnership? Can it carry on any other business?

- Who are the partners? Are they all general partners? Who is the senior partner? Can other people become partners, and, if so, do all the existing partners have to be in favour?

- How much capital is each partner bringing into the partnership? Will the partnership have its own business premises, or will these belong to one or more partners? What is the position with partnership equipment, cars, etc?
  How much interest will the partnership pay each year on the capital? How much rent for the premises, cars, and so on?

- Who is responsible for making contracts for the partnership? Who signs the cheques? Who keeps the books? Does any one partner have unlimited authority to do these things, or do bigger contracts or cheques need signing by two or more partners?

- How much time will each partner spend in the business? What holidays are allowed? What happens if a partner is ill? Are partners allowed to carry on any other business at the same time?

- Who hires and fires the staff? How are other important decisions to be reached? What happens if there is a dispute between the partners?

- How long does the partnership last? What happens if a partner wants to retire? Do the other partners pay a pension? How much notice is needed to leave the partnership, or to take capital out?

- What happens if one partner dies? Will the partnership survive? Are the other partners aware of their liabilities? (The deceased partner's dependants can demand their share of the partnership – in cash.) Should cross-partnership life policies be a condition?

Co-operatives

Co-operatives are somewhere between employment and self-employment. They are businesses where, technically, the workforce are all employees of the co-operative, but where the same people are also the employer. In many partnerships as in a company some of those involved are more equal than others. In a co-operative everyone is genuinely equal. They are all running their own business even though, inevitably, they have different jobs to do within the business. Some co-operatives are very small. Others, like the John Lewis Partnership, can be national names.

Co-operatives sometimes emerge when businesses are to close but the staff agree to club together (often pooling redundancy money) to get the business from the employer and run it jointly. Quite often members are pulled together by a common ideal in the true workers co-operative. ICOM, the **Industrial Common Ownership Movement** (address at end) exists to encourage worker co-operatives, and helps with information, and access to finance. Co-operatives need to register and adopt certain formalities, and ICOM helps with these.

A Government agency, the **Co-operative Development Agency** (address at end) promotes the interests of co-operatives, with limited powers to make grants and loans. In some areas there are also **local co-operative development agencies**, often supported by local councils, and they may be the best place for help if near you. Find out through the CDA.

Companies

There are several kinds of company, including unlimited companies, and companies limited by guarantee. Only one sort is important to the small business, the **company limited by shares** or **Co Ltd** as we normally say. A **plc** (public limited company) is the special status for the large publicly owned company, which we ignore here. The key to a limited company is that the company belongs to the people who have shares in it, or its **shareholders**. Their liability is to the company, not its customers, for the full value of the shares, and no more.

The crucial difference between running a business as a sole trader or through a partnership, and through a company is that in law the company is separate from those who own it. It is the company, not the company's owners, which runs the business. This means that if the business fails, the company will fail but not its shareholders, who lose only the value of the shares. That, at any rate, is the theory. In practice, it doesn't quite work that simply in most cases.

How is a company formed?

A company can be set up only through the **Companies Registration Office** (address at end). To register a company, the intending shareholders must draw up and file a series of documents setting out the company's rules, and details about it and its owners. The key documents of any company are:

- the **Memorandum** setting out the company's 'vital statistics':
  - name
  - country of registration (England or Scotland)
  - objects and purposes of the business
  - total value of the share capital.
- the **Articles of Association** setting out the company's rules.

This can be a long, complex document, but often follows a

standard form laid down in **Table A,** rules laid down under the Companies Act 1985, the main law on companies.

Along with these documents, the Registration Office must receive the name(s) of the first **directors** and secretary of the company. All companies must have either two directors or a director and a company secretary. There must also be two **subscribers**, people who will buy at least one share each. A company must always have two shareholders – though one can be a nominee of the other (for instance the main shareholder's solicitor), so in reality one-man companies are easily set up.

The company's **name** must be different from that of any other company – have some spare names at hand. A name can be changed once the company is in existence but the country of registration cannot be changed.

The company's **objects** are vital, as these set the legal limits to the powers of the company's management to carry on business. Action outside the company's powers is said to be beyond its powers or **ultra vires.** A company can sometimes refuse to carry out a contract made in excess of its actual powers. This is usually so where a company makes an ultra vires agreement with its owners and directors, and can create serious problems for the owners if a company becomes insolvent or gets into the hands of others. The objects need to be drafted with care.

The company's **rules** are usually of little concern to outsiders, but are as important as the partnership agreement to the owners and directors. Many of the questions in the partnership checklist will also apply to setting limits to the directors' powers and duties, and the holding of meetings. There will also be rules about selling the company's shares – usually preventing outsiders getting hold of company shares without agreement of at least a majority of existing shareholders.

You can set up a company by buying one 'off the shelf'. They are advertised regularly in the business press for about £180 or so. It is usually wiser to get either your solicitor or a company registration agent to set one up to your requirements, and to get them to explain the legal requirements of a company for you, as the Companies Act lays down in considerable detail the rights and duties of the directors, shareholders, company secretary and others, and requires regular **annual returns** of information about the company.

Running a company

Once the registration certificate is issued, the subscribers take up their shares to become shareholders, and the company holds its first meeting to appoint one or more directors and a secretary. It is then required to elect company auditors (the business's accountants do this), and select a registered office (usually the accountants' or solicitors' office), and is in business.

Just as a company's formation has to follow a set form by law, so does its running. The company is required to have an **AGM** for its shareholders within 18 months of the start, and at least every 15 months afterwards. These meetings must receive (and hopefully approve) reports from the directors and auditors, and elect directors and the auditors. **Annual reports** must include summaries of the accounts, names of the directors, details about the shareholders, and other information. Further, a copy of these details must be filed each year as an **annual return** to the Companies Registration Office. There they are open to public inspection, and will be monitored and scrutinised by potential rivals and predators.

This may seem a lot of formality for a one-man business, but these legal requirements cannot be ignored. Equally, it is advisable if there are two or more people involved to keep proper, if short, minutes of all formal decisions of the directors and meetings.

Keeping the company separate

With a small business, it is difficult to keep the company's affairs separate from those of its owner in what is in effect a one-person business. Company property must be kept separate from the shareholders' property. It must trade in its own name, not its owner's; keep separate bank accounts, books and contracts. Its owner will be an employee for income tax and social security purposes (see Chapter 14, 'Your share, their share') if he or she works for the business, even as managing director and sole employee. As we shall see below, the owner can instead take out the money as dividends on the shares, and the possibilities will depend in part on taxation questions.

What form of business?

There are both advantages and disadvantages in running a business through a company rather than a partnership, and no one clear answer as to what form a business should adopt. Obviously the big businesses are nearly always companies (apart from accountants and lawyers, who are not allowed as yet to be incorporated), whilst the very smallest businesses will often find the corporate form very formal. The following points may help you decide.

Checklist: What form of business?

- **Setting up** Should involve formality for a partnership. Must involve formalities and official fees for a company. Nothing for a sole trader.
- **Running costs** Minimal for a partnership, and none for a sole trader, but the company must throughout comply with all legal requirements.
- **Changing your mind** Whilst it is fairly easy to turn an unincorporated business into a company, the reverse is not true, and can be very expensive for tax reasons – so don't rush into forming a company. Ask your advisors.
- **Image** Don't be taken in by the glamour of being a company director – others won't be. On balance the business may look a more serious endeavour if incorporated.
- **Secrecy** A partnership reports 'nuffin' to no one'. A company has to publish part of its accounts and other key details.
- **Accounts and auditing** The partnership keeps its figures secret, whilst a company must publish the main details. Company accounts must be officially audited, while there are no requirements imposed on partnership accounts for outsiders.
- **Borrowing money** It is easier for a company to raise money than a partnership, whose main source will be loans. Companies can get investments through selling some shares, and there are tax schemes to help this, or by raising money by a floating charge (see Chapter 11, 'Raising cash').
- **Limited liability** There is no limit to the liability of general partners of a partnership, or sole traders. In principle, the shareholders of a limited company risk only their invested capital. But in practice, banks, landlords and others will demand personal guarantees from the company's owners (see Chapter 11, 'Raising cash').
- **Tax** There are several different tax reasons why you may wish to be or not to be a company – summarised below.
- **Social security and pensions** Because all those in the business are treated as employees they pay the higher Class 1 contributions while partners pay Classes 2 and 4. Private pension schemes for employees and partners have similar terms.
- **Selling or passing on your interest** Because the company is legally separate from its owners it is easier to sell the business, especially part of it, or to pass a share in the business to other members of the family for personal or tax reasons.

Some tax points

For small businesses it is often better for tax reasons not to be incorporated. This is because:

- **Income tax** – Where there is a company, its employees pay tax on their earnings under the less generous employee rules – but taxation of perks may be better for employees. A company pays flat rate tax at 25% or 35% and, if it keeps its trading income, pays no more, while if it is earned by a partner, or given by a company to its employees or shareholders, they will pay higher rate tax on it. So this can work both ways.

- **National insurance contributions** are much higher on employees including, of course, the employers' contribution. This may be avoided in some cases by paying dividends to the owners rather than earnings.

- **Capital gains** – This works one way only. Companies and their owners get taxed twice on capital gains. The company pays on making the gain. But this increases the share value to the owner, who will pay gains tax on selling or giving the shares on that gain. At 25% gains tax and 25% company tax, that makes a combined charge of 44%, while individuals never pay more than 40%, with several generous exemptions. It is also one reason why it can be expensive to disincorporate a successful business – it forces a gains tax charge on the shares.

- **Stamp duty** – This is also one way only. There is a 1% stamp duty on all sales of shares (at least until 1991). There is no stamp duty in moving partners' capital into or out of a partnership.

- **Inheritance tax** and **tax planning** – It is far easier to make gifts of shares to reduce inheritance tax liabilities than move a share of an unincorporated business.

6 Plan it

If you don't know where you're going, you won't get there. Before you set out, it is vital that you know your objectives, and that you plan how to attain them. Whatever your business, big or small, you must have a **business plan** setting out your objectives and how to achieve them. If you don't, you will probably fail to achieve your aims and your business will probably fail altogether. The number one reason for business failure is failure to plan.

The business plan tells you what to do about achieving your objectives. It must be thorough and cover all aspects of what you are doing. That's why most of this book is concerned with aspects of your planning. But the highlights of your plan will be the five Ps. You must **Plan the five Ps:**

PURPOSE PRODUCT POTENTIAL PEOPLE POUNDS

Purpose

What is the aim of your business? What are your objectives in setting it up? This is the core of your plan. Write your aims down in a short, simple statement – six or seven lines should suffice. It should answer the vital issue: where is your business going?

This is crucial to your planning, because it states your principal objectives, and challenges you to channel your energies into those objectives. The rest of the plan is your proposed way of achieving the target, and should prevent you from being side-tracked into irrelevant activities. These merely waste your most valuable resource – you.

Don't be afraid of having to alter the aims later. If you are successful, you will probably need to do so anyway. In any event, you should reconsider the aims every few months to see if they should be revised. As your business develops, so your targets will change.

Only you can set that purpose. Why not have a first try now:

The main objective of my business is

....

....

....

....

....

Product

To achieve your purpose you will provide something for your customers. Your plan should identify what this is. In both Chapter 8, 'What are you selling?' and 'Tell the world', Chapter 9, we look closely at this question, and ask you to name the key advantages of your product. Whatever your business, you must be supplying a product to someone. If you are to succeed, there must be some special reason why your product is worth obtaining. Write those into a **product description** in your plan for each product you aim to produce. Your plan needs to provide three more Ps for each product: **product price**, **product plan** and **product procurement**.

Product price

All products have a unit cost, that is, the cost of producing one item (or for a service, this may be cost per hour of service). Working this out is part of the market planning we examine in Chapter 8, 'What are you selling?'

Product plan

You must also plan the development of the product, and how it will be kept marketable. Each product, like your whole business, and everything else, has its own life cycle. This will follow the form:

BIRTH — GROWTH — MATURITY — DECLINE

Your business, and each product of it, follows this pattern. Your plan should aim to support the earlier stages for each product, so that decline is postponed. When it comes, the business should have other products at earlier stages of their lives, so the business itself continues to grow.

Decline, when it comes, may be sudden. It may hit not just your product, but a whole industry. If you are tied to one product, you go when it goes. You need to aim for a portfolio of products to protect your business against this threat. If you don't think it a threat, look what happened to the Swiss watch industry a few years ago, or the British shipbuilding industry . . .

Product procurement

Next, you must plan how you will be able to supply your product to your customers. You need to analyse the work involved in preparing everything so that the product is delivered at the right time, place and price. This is your job. But what exactly is it you must do?

Work out a chart, a **Work Breakdown Structure**, of what needs doing, first by the main kinds of activity involved, then splitting down each area of activity. This assists you in planning and then monitoring the business, spotting weak points in your organisation. Try something along the lines of the example opposite.

Along the bottom of your work breakdown structure should be a list of all the activities in which you need to engage to get your product to the market. Does this cover all you should be doing? Have irrelevant activities crept in?

Time it right

Next, you can turn this into a time-organising chart. Each activity in developing your product takes time. What is that time? Can you write it down? Some of those activities must take place before others can be started, whilst some can be done at the same time as others, and some come at the end. What is the best order for them?

If your business involves a chain of activities (as all manufacturing does), a good way of tracing the timing of the activities is to chart them on a **Network Plan**. One way of doing this is shown below. Each activity is represented by a line with circles indicating where the activity begins and is finished. The length of the line helps indicate the time spent on the activity.

This chart gives you other vital information: the length of time each job will take. It shows what is called the **critical path**, the shortest time between the beginning and end of the job. If anything in the critical path goes wrong, the whole job is delayed. Shorten the critical path, and the job gets finished more quickly. Pay careful attention to every aspect of your business on the critical path, and plan to keep them all as short as possible.

The plan also tells you in what order you should be doing

Work Breakdown Structure: The Small Building Co

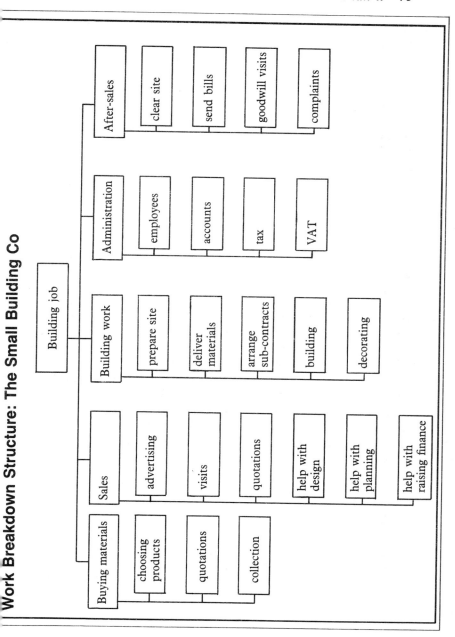

Network chart: Wibble Widgets Ltd – batch of custom-designed widgets

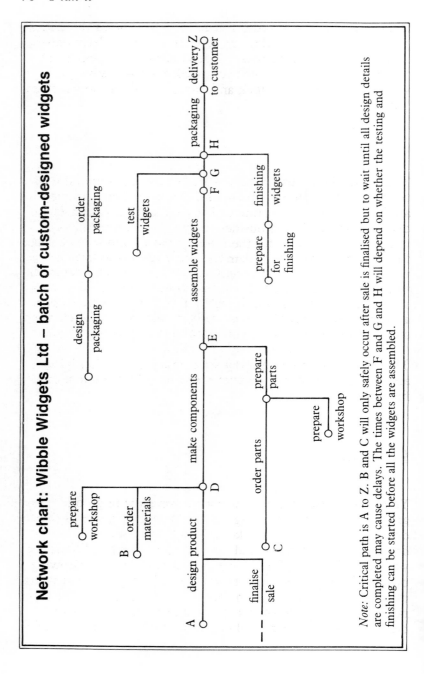

Note: Critical path is A to Z. B and C will only safely occur after sale is finalised but to wait until all design details are completed may cause delays. The times between F and G and H will depend on whether the testing and finishing can be started before all the widgets are assembled.

things. The aim is to order things so as to shorten the critical path as much as possible, but may allow you to delay non-critical parts of the business. This is particularly important to avoid tying up cash until you need to do so. When do you need to buy your stock and equipment? Aim to get them **'just in time'**.

'Just in time'

The principle of 'just in time' is to reduce to a minimum the time during which equipment and materials – and people – are left standing idle before or between jobs. If materials are delivered too early the business may suffer in several ways: it has to pay too soon for the stock; it has to find storage space for it; it runs the risk of damage, theft and deterioration whilst it is lying idle. Getting the stock just in time demands two things of the business – good planning and good suppliers. If the planning is right, it may be cheaper to pay a little more for reliable stock delivery than to go for cheaper supplies which lie around the place 'just in case'.

The same principle applies to staff time – is that left lying around, or do staff get on with a second job as the first one finishes?

Potential

Your plan must explore how your business is to go on growing. If it stops growing, it will be mature and will then decline. This involves market research and product development as discussed above and in Chapter 8, 'What are you selling?' and is further covered in Chapter 16, 'Growing bigger'. The business plan should include targets for growing in either of the ways shown there – by expanding the product range to existing customers, or expanding the customer bank. It should also be looking to improve the efficiency of the business within its existing product range and customer bank. This will tend to happen in any event as the business moves from the birth phase to the growth phase, but should be monitored carefully.

People

Another part of the plan is you and the other people involved in the business. As the business grows, so will the number of people involved. You need to recruit with care, and plan who does what in the business. Everyone in the team will also need to be managed. Remember, they are your biggest asset next to yourself, and should be given the opportunity to contribute their maximum to the business, and to get the maximum out of it. This is discussed in Chapter 15, 'Being the boss'.

Pounds

The other element vital to your business plan is the cash. You must plan thoroughly all the financial aspects of your business. This involves budgeting ahead for the capital needed to start up the business (see Chapter 11, 'Raising cash'), and for the cash flow position of the business month by month (see below). Further, you should be budgeting for the projected profits of the business on the basis of your objectives, and the potential you aim to exploit in the coming year (also discussed below). Finally, you should work out the actual and estimated unit costs of your products (see above and Chapter 8, 'What are you selling?').

All these financial projections of the business together give you a good picture of what is supposed to be happening. Your records and management accounting have the purpose of making sure you stay on target or, if you are missing the target, of alerting you to the change so that you can take corrective action.

Cash flow

Cash flow means the money coming into and going out of the business week by week. Most businesses are seasonal so, unlike a wage packet, profits will come in unevenly. Perhaps a large customer refrains from paying for two months. And the bills come in unevenly too. Problems arise the moment bills have to be paid faster than profits come in – as far too many small builders learn to their cost. It is no good knowing that when you complete a new house, you will make a massive profit, if you can't afford to pay the tiler to put the roof on.

It is absolutely fundamental to every business – and all personal expenditure too – that cash flow must always be in control. Once it gets out of control, disaster awaits. For far too many businesses during the first three years, that is why they fail. Basic advance planning reduces this risk.

What you need is more work for your pencil – a **cash flow forecast**. There's an example below, to show what can go wrong. You can get blank forms for your own forecast from your local bank – otherwise adapt the basic form used here.

It is standard practice in accounts to put negative figures in brackets, so we can see Flo's business is in the red.

Flo's projections show that she has no ready cash until after August, and is heavily in the red for three months. How could she have avoided this, without in any way increasing her income? What would have happened if she had secured the loan a month earlier, and had put off some of the expenditure (eg the capital items and repairs) for a couple of months? This is a simple example, but when you have your own cash

Flo's Angling Supplies: cash flow forecast (from start in May)

	May	June	July	August
Starting balance	0	(4800)	(3400)	(2200)
Income:				
cash sales	1000	1500	2500	2500
credit sales	–	1000	2000	2000
capital receipts	–	5000	–	–
other income	100	200	200	200
Total income	**1100**	**7700**	**4700**	**4900**
Outgoings:				
cash purchases	200	100	100	100
credit purchases	2000	500	500	–
wages, etc	1000	1000	1000	1000
rent and rates	1000	1000	1000	1000
running premises	300	–	300	–
repairs etc	1000	–	–	–
running equipment	200	200	200	200
travel	100	200	100	100
capital purchases	–	3000	–	–
loan payments	–	200	200	200
other expenses	100	100	100	100
Total expenses	**5900**	**6300**	**3500**	**2700**
Balance for month	(4800)	1400	1200	2200
CLOSING BALANCE	**(4800)**	**(3400)**	**(2200)**	**0**

flow projection, look at the alternatives it suggests, plus the amount of start up capital needed.

Budgeting

You should also be looking ahead to your intended profit level. This is a separate exercise to the cash flow forecast because the profits calculation is based on earnings, rather than when cash comes in. You should check this in the same way as cash flow, producing a best guess at the profit and loss account for the month, and so on for the current year.

Have a look at the profit and loss account in 'Control your cash' and compare it with the cash flow form. What you need to check here is:

1		Sales (turnover)
2	*minus*	cost of sales
3	*plus*	other income *gives*
4		GROSS PROFIT (1 – 2 + 3)
5	*minus*	overheads
6		NET PROFIT (4 – 5)
7		CUMULATIVE NET PROFIT (total at 6 plus same for each previous month of year)

The budget forecast will be different from the cash flow figures. It also emphasises a fundamental difference between the **fixed overheads** and the **variable** (or sales-related) **overheads**. That is important in working out the **break-even point** for the business. This is because you must pay the fixed overheads whatever your sales, whilst on each sale your gross profit is the difference between the sale proceeds and the cost of that sale. Once you work that out, you know what your minimum sales must be to cover all overheads.

Spotting trouble coming

Clearly the budget must take into account the break-even figure and show a sensible profit as the target. How to get to that target is, of course, part of the business plan. But you must also check how you are actually doing compared with the budget and also roll the whole process forward every

month, as you should do with the cash flow forecast. That
way you can see as soon as possible when either cash flow or
profit predictions are going wrong, and can start corrective
action.

Putting the plan together

Once you have planned the five Ps, construct your full
business plan to cover everything from your long term
objectives to a detailed monthly estimate of your financial
position. You may need two or more business plans. The
fullest one is for your use. But when you need to raise money,
lenders want to see a business plan, and all the information
about product, potential, people and pounds we explored
above. Set out the information you have assembled in
preparing your own plan. Start it with a short general
description of your business and the market of which your
business is part. Prepare the document carefully and you have
a good argument why the bank should lend you the money
you need.

7 Go where?

Two crucial decisions you will make – possibly by doing nothing – are the location of your business and the kind of premises you base it in. This chapter aims to alert you to thinking about advantages and disadvantages of different locations and buildings.

Moving to the best area

What is 'best' varies enormously between businesses. It is not always where you now are. Many, particularly manufacturers, will have some flexibility of location. For them, economic and financial factors can combine to make some areas most attractive locations because of lower overheads and local financial aid.

Local overheads

The cost of business premises ranges widely around the country. Land and rental prices in London are way above those even an hour out of the capital – whilst in parts of the North and West of the UK you may get a new factory rent-free for some years. This used to be reinforced by the local rates, but in 1990 these were replaced by the National Business Rate, at the same percentage throughout England, with different levels in Wales and Scotland. The total cost depends on the rateable value of each property, which vary throughout the country.

Other overheads also vary, such as labour costs, particularly average weekly pay. This is at its highest in the London travel-to-work area (which extends as far as Oxford), though employees may be better off elsewhere because of much cheaper housing. Services cost more in that area, too.

Moving to the right premises

For a retail business, and for some services, this will be perhaps the most critical part of your planning. It's no good opening up where nobody can find you, or where the double yellow lines (painted by the council just after you arrived) stop all parking. So, it's time for pencil and paper again. Work out what you are looking for before you go hunting. Don't allow yourself to be persuaded something is ideal when it will not do. Some points to consider:

Checklist: Premises

- What premises do you need – workshop, office, store, shop, garage, other?
- How big should they be?
- Where should they be – High Street, side street, ground level, upstairs, doesn't matter?
- Do all the premises have to be together?
- What extra facilities will your business need?
- How important is appearance – to customers, to your employees, to you?
- What should it cost – rent or mortgage, rates, service charges, running costs, alterations, repairs?

Local help

Financial help and advice is available for small businesses
from Government and local councils and some private
sources to encourage or protect businesses in specified areas.
Contact the local enterprise agency or the Small Firms
Service for the full story for your area. The following lists
key kinds of support available.

Government aid

By special tax reliefs – Businesses based in an **Enterprise
Zone** pay no rates for several years and get full capital
allowances for tax purposes on business building costs. This
means that the full cost of new buildings can be set against
corporation or income tax. There are 25 EZs, usually in city
centres or areas of de-industrialisation. They have other
advantages, such as relaxed planning procedures, and
exemption from industrial training levies.

Import and export businesses may find some help from
organising their transportation through a **Freeport**,
providing postponement of customs duty and VAT until
goods leave the freeport, plus relaxation of some formalities.

The only offset otherwise available against tax are grants paid
in **Northern Ireland** only to offset the cost of corporation tax
on certain projects.

By grants – Smaller businesses setting up in or moving to an
Assisted Area are entitled to seek capital grants from the
DTI. Other grants are paid as **Regional Selective Assistance**
in both the assisted areas, and additional **Intermediate
Areas**, by way of project grants and training grants. These
help projects designed to increase or protect employment in

the area. These grants are administered by the **Regional Development Grant Offices** of the DTI (Department of Trade and Industry). Separate schemes apply in **Scotland, Wales** and **Northern Ireland**.

Aid from local councils

Local authorities have powers to help small businesses get established in their areas, though they vary widely as to how they do this. One programme aims at helping the **Inner Urban Areas**, and funds are available for inner city developments. Councils within the scope of the Inner Urban Area funds are able to support a wide variety of both commercial and non-profit schemes designed to improve the local economy and environment.

More generally, councils can give valuable advice, backed in some cases by material assistance in the form of grants, loans or, sometimes, low-cost factory units and help with housing. The varying but tight budget restraints on councils mean that local funding of business initiatives may be limited. Some councils devote their attention to making sure you know they are (or think they are) at the centre of things – but seem to have spent all their budget on advertising when you ask for help. Others do less advertising, but provide solid advice when you find them. Ask around.

Get permission

Wherever you choose to go, make sure you have permission for what you intend to do. No new building can be erected or other works started, and no existing building can be used in a materially different way from its present use, without **planning permission** from the local council. Local councils use planning permission to prevent people using land in ways the council does not want, so you will find limits on where you can start your business. In practice, you can use land for the same broad range of uses as its current use (provided, of course, that is legal). So, a shop can be used for selling most kinds of goods without extra planning permission.

You may also need the permission of the landowner, if you are a tenant. Even if you own the land, it may be subject to **restrictive covenants** which may prevent you using the land the way you want to. These are limits placed on uses of freehold land by a previous owner. If worried, your solicitor will advise.

New buildings – and alterations – must comply with the **building regulations** supervised by the local council. Architects and builders should take these into account in any work they do, but plans will need to be sent to the local council for approval, in addition to any plans needed for planning permission.

Buy or rent?

While ideally it is best, in the long term, to own most premises as an investment, this may prove too costly, may tie you down too tightly or may be impossible because no freehold premises are available, and you will need to rent. A lease is simply buying time in someone else's property, usually on their terms. The crucial points are – how much, and for how long? The cost can come in several ways – a premium or lump sum for the right to buy the lease; rent on a regular basis, and which will no doubt increase from time to time (watch when the next rent review is due), and service charges for landlord's maintenance and other costs (watch how that is worked out). The time bought may be just a week at a time, or a fixed period of several years – check this. Which is best in your interests?

If renting, watch two sets of rules, one working for you, the other usually against you. The set working against you are the restrictions in the **lease** or renting agreement. Leases can be fearsome legal documents, and it is wise to seek a solicitor's advice on its contents.

The set working for you are the **Landlord and Tenant Acts**. Just as private tenants are protected by law from the excesses of their landlords, so are business tenants. Legal requirements must be met before tenants can be given notice to quit, and sometimes landlords have to pay compensation. Proper procedures must be followed when the rent is increased. It's worth getting legal advice then too.

8 What are you selling?

I ask this because, although it is the wrong question with which to start, nonetheless many people work out a very positive answer to it. They should have been working on their answer to another question. That is:

What can you provide that other people want to buy and are prepared to pay for?

The difference between the questions is the difference between **marketing** your business and abilities, and **selling** your existing or intended range of products or services. Sure, you need to sell yourself. That's why the next chapter ('Tell the world') is devoted to it. But that still assumes that someone wants to buy what you are selling. Do you know that, and do you know who wants to buy? Just as important, do you know why they want to buy?

Your planning should include much more than deciding how you are going to sell your product. Find out what customers really want, and how much it will cost to give them what they want, then make sure you can get it to them. Only then does the selling start. Before that we must concentrate on market research, product planning and product pricing. This is all more work for your pencil.

Well, what *are* you selling?

By this stage you probably have a fairly clear idea of the line of business you intend to enter – either something you will create or manufacture, or a particular area of sales or supply of services. Your objective should be to identify what you aim to supply. Of course, you can perfectly properly start at the other end, without a clear idea, and go looking for something in which to trade. After all, any line of business which produces a profit is a line worth pursuing by someone.

The essence is to realise the range of things that you can provide, and see what will work best. Unless you are a sub-contractor aiming to supply one or a very few main contractors, you have some scope for adjusting what you are doing. If you are an expert you can sell both products and expertise, by becoming the local specialist. Or you can offer extra efficiency or speed in delivery. Or go the other way and provide a 'no frills' service.

Generally small businesses survive on providing that extra 'something' customers want and which big businesses find it much harder or too expensive to supply. That's why it is important to identify the market for which you are catering – and to check it out.

Researching the market

There are two parts to researching your proposed customers: **library research**, that is, finding out from the wealth of information available everything you can about your customers, your competitors, and likely developments amongst both; and **direct research** or, to quote someone recently, 'Get on yer bike' and go and find out.

Get the data together

Whatever specialist market you enter, there is a wealth of published knowledge available about the market just waiting for you to take a systematic look through it. There are two ways to get at this: via your local reference library, or via your local enterprise agency or the Small Firms Service. Some libraries (Hampshire, for example) produce special guides to help – and the staff invariably will do so.

Population figures are kept in the **Registrar General's** annual reports, whilst information about spending comes from the annual **Family Expenditure Surveys**. And there is much more. The **Census of Distribution** for your local area will tell you how many similar sorts of shops there are in your area, and what their overall profitability is. And the DTI's **Business Monitors** give regular updates on the state of the markets for many different sectors of the economy. A huge range of statistics are available in national or local statistical collections.

You can supplement this data from several sources. There are a large number of commercially prepared directories which will give you all the names and addresses you need for suppliers, competitors, relevant organisations, and so on. Professional organisations and trade associations have membership lists, many of them published. And, of course, there are telephone directories, **Yellow Pages** being a most valuable reference source.

You should look out for specialist journals, of which a good commercial library should stock a selection. Find out what journals and papers are available in your trade, and get hold of copies. If you are not sure, check in **British Rate and Data**, which is the list of all journals, papers and periodicals produced for advertisers. There may well also be relevant specialist books in the reference part of the library. Check your nearest business library via the library catalogue (or the library staff).

Another approach to finding out what you want is through **trade exhibitions** and **conferences**. The specialist exhibitions like the regional Ideal Home exhibitions, or the Business to Business displays give you a splendid chance to see what others are up to, and to talk to both suppliers and customers. That should give you some ideas for selling, as well.

From all these sources, you should be assembling data on what the market looks like, how it is changing, how the national picture is reflected in your region, and what your potential competitors are doing about meeting market demand, and even roughly how much money they are making at it.

If your competitors are companies, you can get more information about them, because (as we have already seen in Chapter 5, 'Two's a company') all companies have to file information about themselves. This is available to you via a **company search** at the Companies Registration Office (commercial agencies do this for you quite cheaply) or, more readily, via the company information services such as Extel which major business libraries carry.

File it

Finally, do not neglect the information you can pick up as you go along, keeping cuttings out of the press, leaflets and advertisements from rivals or information about the customers you intend to serve. Keep that, along with all the other information you have gleaned, in an organised way and it will well repay the time spent gathering it.

Test the market

Most of the information collected so far can be gained without venturing into the marketplace in any sense (except, anonymously if you wish, at the trade exhibitions). Now go and find out what people want. Ask your friends and contacts. Ask those who you think you will be supplying what they would like. Ask your own intended suppliers what they think. Most people are flattered to be asked their advice. It is paying them a compliment to listen to their experience, and they usually return the compliment by telling you what they think will serve you well.

Depending on what your business is, you can do your own, or commission the experts to do, market research in the well-tried Gallup method of asking organised questions. If that is what you want, it is important to ensure that the questions you ask do not get so loaded that they produce only loaded answers, and also that the questions are organised to find out what you want to know. In practice that sort of level of research is way beyond what many small businesses need, and beyond their budgets. They can get what they want by systematic desk work backed by listening to those whom they have approached informally.

Keep monitoring

Once you have started, there will be a steady source of market information available to your from within your own business. It is vital to keep tabs on that. What are people buying from you, when (time of day/year) do they buy? Are they buying for themselves or others? If you have credit customers, keep a note of all present and past customers, and what they buy. Or keep a check on who comes into your office or shop during a set period, so as to get a full picture.

Complaints are good for you

Check what goes wrong even more carefully. Many retailers
have gained in market share simply by noting the things
people ask for that are not in stock, and spotting additional
opportunities. Then look to the complaints. However good
you are, you will get complaints and grumbles from
customers. You are too slow, too quick, badly stocked,
carrying so many lines it is confusing, too dear, too cheap.

We all receive complaints, and we all dislike it. But the wiser
people are those who get better because of their mistakes,
regarding them as suggestions for improvement rather than
personal insults. Few people enjoy complaining (and we soon
find out those that do!), so when they complain there is a
good reason. If someone complains, how many other
customers could have complained but did not? Perhaps the
complaint is aimed at your rivals too. There's a new market
opportunity.

Don't neglect your staff, once they are in post. They are the
people that have to grin stupidly whilst getting roundly cursed
because you forgot the customer's order. And they like to
have their opinion heard too – what is more, they probably
know what they are talking about, and will certainly know
what their friends think of your business.

Product planning

By now your pencil should have done a fair amount of work
finding out about the market. Use that to your best advantage
by planning how best to exploit the market. You should have
a better idea of what people think they want, and what the
competition currently offers them.

Think about the demand you are intending to supply from the customer's point of view. Your (or my) literary masterpiece may be viewed by the reader as a reasonably pleasant dose of anaesthetic to ward off the effects of one of British Rail's less efficient services. (It was noticeable, when I was doing some of my own market research, how many business books are now sold through the bookshops at stations and airports – why?) The grotty room at the back of a small hotel on the Costa Grigia will be romanticised into sunshine, cheap booze and scope for late night exercise. The banana peeling machine you so cleverly invented is the way for Fred Ltd to sack an overpaid and unpopular operative as redundant.

Within your intended market, there is room for choice. You should know what your competitors are supplying. They will of course react to your presence if they can. How are you going to compete with them and grab your market share? They have the advantage of being there first – or is it a disadvantage? Your research should give you an answer to that. Is their delivery time so unreliable that people will pay more for guaranteed delivery? Or is it the sort of place where you pay for excessive attention that most customers don't want, or where they need advice but can't readily get it, or where goods are sometimes faulty, but the supplier is very stroppy when customers ask for money back?

Here again, keep your pencil busy. Work out the options, and the different levels at which you could supply the market. And if you supply them with one thing, why not with other compatible goods or services?

What will it cost?

At the same time as working out what the customers want, you need to work out what it will cost to supply it. If you can also find out what the customers are prepared to pay (what do your rivals charge?), then you have a good indication of the profitability of your business.

Costing is the other side of the operation we have looked at in Chapter 6, 'Plan it', of building up a cash flow projection and profit budget, along with the start-up budget and other figures we look at in Chapter 11, 'Raising cash' and the figures we will chase in Chapter 12, 'Control your money', in particular those which will fix the break-even point of the business.

Overheads

Your business will incur two kinds of overheads whatever you intend to supply. First, the **fixed overheads** such as the cost of buying or renting the premises. You must pay these whether or not you sell anything. Then there are the **sales-related** or variable overheads, or the cost of supplying each item of goods or service.

It is most important to monitor these once you get going, but you also need to do a bit of intelligent guessing before you start, to make sure you get your pricing right. Costing time can be harder than costing production of, say, a dozen stock items. But it is still calculable.

How much an hour?

The starting point is the hourly (or monthly) rate of charge of the member of staff. In your own case, it is how much an hour you intend to make for your efforts. The rate you will have to charge customers will need to be higher than this, to take account of non-charged hours, fixed overheads, payroll costs and so on.

For example, Fred is paid £5 an hour for a 40 hour week, plus £7.50 for overtime. What will be his charge rate, assuming he is attending charged calls for 80 per cent of his time?

Total charged time:
32 hours a week for (say) 47 weeks (allowing for holidays) = 1504 hours (say 1500).
Total cost of employing Fred (excluding overtime):
£200 a week plus employer's NI contributions and other direct staff costs, say, £25 a week, for 52 weeks = £11700.
Direct cost per hour:
£11700 over 1500 hours = £7.80 per hour.

To this we need to add overheads tied up in making Fred's services available. He may have a van permanently at his disposal, plus a full range of spare parts and an extensive tool kit. Then there is the back-up service of accounts, making appointments and so forth. Assume Fred is one of two people employed by the business. The total overhead cost of what they are doing, on an annual basis, is £15,000, allowing for full cost of vans, and all office costs. Fred's share is £7,500 which, spread over his chargeable 1500 hours, means his rate must go up to £12.80 an hour to break even. Your profit margin is to be added to that. Small wonder that so many firms now have call-out fees of £15 or more.

Costing goods

If you are producing goods, work out the cost of each item by reference to the length of charged time you and any staff spend on the item, plus the direct costs of producing it. Again, the profit margin comes on at the end.

If Fred and similarly paid staff were producing items, they would probably be productively employed for more than 32 hours a week (though no doubt less than 40), so the charge rate including all overheads might be, say, £10 an hour. If it takes four hours work to produce one item, using raw materials worth £5, the item costs £45 to produce before allowing for profit, contingencies, and so on.

Cost price and market price

Don't confuse the cost of goods (plus desired profit margin) with the price. What price you can charge depends much less on you than your customers. That is, unless you can get yourself a monopoly for an essential item, which is the privilege only of businesses like the Post Office or specialist firms who are so competitive in their pricing that nobody else can compete with them for their small market.

What the customers want to pay may have little to do with the cost. For example, they may be prepared to pay twice as much for a reliable service than one which delivers the goods erratically. Yet it may cost you only a little extra to gear your firm to guarantee delivery.

Take Fred, for example. His ordinary hourly rate is over £12, but, paradoxically, his hourly charge rate for overtime is less than that. Whilst he gets paid more (and up go the payroll costs), we are recovering all the fixed overhead costs against his ordinary charged hours, so these do not affect overtime hours. But it is a fair bet that customers will more readily pay a higher call-out charge if Fred is prepared to turn out in the evening to sort out their problem than for an ordinary daytime call.

Persuading the customers to pay more whenever Fred turns out is the theme of the next chapter.

What was it you were selling?

If your pencil has been kept busy you will now have a much better answer to my original question (though it may not be the same one as that with which you started). This is because you can answer some other questions with more confidence: what do the buyers want? Who are they, and why are they buying? What can I supply them with, and what will it cost me to do so?

9 Tell the world

Your product is very good value for money. It is an excellent product and you are a person with whom any sensible customer will want to do business. This is because you know what your customers want, and you know you can supply it the way they want it. You have done your market research and your product planning, and you know that these statements are true. But do the customers know that? Probably not, so – go tell them. Tell as many of them as you can. After all, you are doing them a favour. How do you best do that?

A checklist for success

First, another job for your pencil. Get a sheet of paper, and write on it all possible advantages customers can gain from your product. You want to list all the answers you can think of to this question:

My customers will want to buy this because

....

....

....

....

....

Engage in a bit of brain-storming. Write down everything that comes to mind, however daft it might sound. Even better, get one or two others to help you do this, so you feed off each other's ideas. If you find your list a bit short, perhaps a bit more product planning is called for, eg, so you can say 'It looks nice' or whatever. Add to the list all the facilities that go with your product – pleasant service, prompt delivery, out-of-hours repair service. Look at every aspect of what you are selling and how you are selling it.

If you run out of ideas, find how others are selling similar products. How do they let the world know how good they are? You should already know, because in your market research you should have accumulated details of all your rivals' products. If you have not, it is still not too late!

When your list is complete, you have your checklist for success. Somewhere in this list is what your customers want to hear, and the best reason for buying from you. But a word of warning. Keep the list completely honest. Do not try and fool anyone. You want your customers to stay good customers. If your product is not worth having, it needs changing. Do not pretend advertising will solve all your problems. Change the product, or its price.

Now write a much shorter list. Put in this list the very best reasons for buying from you. What you are after are your unique selling points, even if there is only one. Your USPs are the points about your product that you can offer, but no one else can, to your customers. Which brings us to the next list.

The wanted persons list

Who will buy? Hold on! That's not a new question. No – but we now need the answer. In reality, the whole world will not want to buy, though they may all need telling, so your customers hear your message. Somewhere out there are *your* customers, and you now need to write down as clearly as you can who they are. The more specific your description, the better. Just like the police, until you have a good description, you don't stand much chance of catching those you are after.

How to spread the good news

We now have the ammunition and the target. How do we hit that target? In advertising, as on a shooting range, there are many ways of doing this. There can be the long-distance telescopic rifle with night sights, the machine gun, or even the anti-tank missile. Or, if you like, there can be the hard sell salesman, the newspaper advertisement, or the sort of spiel we get from politicians at election time. All work well on the right customers.

Which are the weapons for you? Forget television; it costs far too much. Likewise forget the national newspapers' full-page ads. Your publicity budget does not allow you to think that big, even though those forms of advertisement can be extremely effective. But so is much more modest local advertising. Here are some more realistic alternatives:

- *Local newspapers* – Both the weeklies and, increasingly, the free local papers. They, in particular, live by advertising so will be only too keen to help you advertise through them.
- *Small ads* in national papers, particularly at the weekends or in specialist features. Similarly ads in the specialist journals for your trade will help. There's a complete guide to this sort of advertising, called British Rate and Data. Check it in your local library. It tells you the key details, including cost and the circulation.
- *Local radio* – If your message should be heard not read, what better?

- **Direct mail** – Post your message as a letter or leaflet to everyone you can find who fits your 'wanted person' description. This is said to be the most effective form of advertising, *providing* you have the right mailing list. That you can get from those same directories we discussed in 'Getting the data together', Chapter 8 – or telephone directories. If you want a complete list of everyone in a certain area, get the electoral register from the local council.

  However be careful not to mail too many people as postage costs are not insignificant. If you only get a 1% reply to your direct mailshot then effectively you will have to stand 100 times the postage cost for each reply. There are several ways of selecting your target audience as mentioned but the Royal Mail offer a Household Delivery Service which starts at a 1,000 letters and a new service called Mailsort which is a discount bulk service for 4,000 letters and above which in effect reduces your postage costs for letters sorted into postcode order. Another helpful service is the Mailing Preference Service at 1 New Burlington Street, London W1X 5FD. This service will avoid you mailing any particular addresses where people have already indicated that they do not wish to receive any direct mail. If you are thinking of buying a mailing list from someone else, ask them if it has been 'cleaned up' by the MPS.

- **Telephone directories** – particularly Yellow Pages. Get your entries in as soon as possible, as you may have to wait several months for the new directory to appear.

- **Exhibitions** – Goods which have a local appeal or are made out of local materials will often sell well at exhibitions and trade shows. You can find out more information from two useful publications: the Craftsman's Directory and the Showman's Directory available from Mint Street, Godalming, Surrey (Tel: 0486 822184).

- **Telephone sales** – This can also be targeted, and is increasingly used as a sales technique on 'cold' calls,

those with no previous contact. But you're selling this
way every time anyone phones. Are you always busy?
Do you have one of those bored, rude telephonists? Or
can you charm them over the wires?

- **Posters** – I'm one of millions who spend their lives staring
at posters on stations, underground trains, buses, taxis,
you name it. And they work, don't they? Your display
does not have to be as elaborate as many of those. But
if your shop is at one end of a shopping street, should not
something at the other end tell your customers where
you are?

- **Leaflets** – You can give these out several ways, by
standing in the street, putting them through letter boxes,
advertising that people who write in will get one, putting
them in the shops, inserting them in local newspapers
or specialist journals. All are used all the time. Like direct
mail, the technique works if the leaflet is designed well.

- **Point of sale displays** – Make sure the product is well
presented where it is going to sell, with support from
posters, leaflets, or a well-designed display. If you are
retailing, your whole shop-front is a big advertisement
of your products and you. If it is dowdy and untidy, can
the customers expect better of you? Why not provide
lots of advertising space for your suppliers to sell their,
and your, wares.

- **Packaging** – The advertising that personally most annoys
me is that which stares at me from the cereal packets
every breakfast time. But the children love them, and
regularly fight over who can read which. How much free
advertising space is provided by you in your house or
office? Is your product one that should be packaged well
so that it gets its place in this free display?

- **Direct selling** – Somehow, Britain has a history of
sneering at its salesmen. Why, I do not know, and one
of the successes of recent governments has been to make
us less inclined to sneer, and more inclined to imitate.
If we don't, someone else will. And if you can't, you need
to get someone who can, whether behind the shop
counter or on the doorstep. You need people who can get
on well with others and size up their customers

accurately. But don't forget to make sure they know exactly why your products are worth buying – and worth them selling.

- *Make your product into news* – The most effective advertising there is comes on News at Ten. Think what those shocking famine films wrung from us in relief aid. That's the extreme case, but think how many others get their products or themselves free advertising by being news. It takes a bit of flair, and someone who does not mind the publicity, but if you can just be different, then you can be news. After all, local journalists have an awful lot of pages to fill in each copy. Even better if what you do has a photograph or two attached – that fills space even faster. Better still if you are going to be a good advertiser. They owe you a favour!

That's over a dozen ways of going about it. Which you choose will depend on your product. If you are running a taxi, make sure you advertise in the phone book, whilst a national ad. might be a crazy waste of money. But is that true of selling package holidays? Whichever way you choose, you also need good copy, that is, wording, design and pictures in your advertising.

Hit 'em hard!

Now your pencil must really go to work. You have to work out your sales message. Remember, you now know exactly whom your advertisement is aimed at, and exactly what it is that they will find best about your product. So, tell them in good, clear, plain English. Make the message attractive, like the product. Choose good, honest headlines. Look at the way the experts advertise to your sort of customer. And think pictures as well. Just as photos liven up the news in the papers, so do cartoons, photos, and logos in the ads.

If this time your pencil fails you, get the experts in.

Advertising agents will help you shape up your campaign, advise you on how and where to advertise, and place those ads or prepare and print those leaflets for you. They'll charge, but perhaps not as much as you think, because they get commission from those selling advertising as well. The advertising staff at the local paper will be able to give a lot of guidance on effective use of their paper, if you ask, as will the local printers.

Get your image right

Whatever you do is part of your advertising. Make sure the 'incidental advertising' gives the right message as well. This covers everything from your stationery to, for example, your waiting room. Have you had to sit for ages on a wooden bench in a doctor's waiting room with only a year old copy of 'Country Life' to keep you company? If the doctor cares that little about his patients whilst they wait to see him, is he going to care any more when examining them? Does your waiting area impress or depress?

Finally, do not neglect your business name and image. Choose and stick to an identity, perhaps backed by a logo or a particular colour you always use for your name. Get something which your customers are going to identify as 'you'. Traditionally, people were proud to call their businesses by their own names. Would it really pay a solicitor' firm to be called Doolittle & Dally?

Talking of solicitors, you should be aware of the laws behind selling, which we look at in the next chapter.

10 Big sales, small print

On page 109 is an invoice received from Shark Supplies for some emergency parts provided for you yesterday. The bill is for over twice as much as you thought (even before adding the extras), and what is more some of the parts didn't work. It cost you another £100 to get the things fitted properly when Dolphin Services put things right this morning. Do you have to pay?

When agreement is reached

The law requires three things (in England – Scottish law is different and should be checked) before accepting that people are legally bound by a contract. There must be an **offer** by someone to do something. That offer must be **accepted** by someone else, and there must be **consideration** given by one party to the other, that is, money or something else of value changes hands. In practice, these things are not problems, but what is a problem is deciding when the contract is made, and what terms are part of it.

A contract is made at the time the offer is accepted, and on the terms then applying. Suppose Shark Supplies had used their 'standard terms' on an invoice sent as a quotation, or offer, by them. You accept, but do so on a similar standard letter, referring to your own standard terms. In that case your letter is the acceptance and your standards terms apply to the contract, not Shark's. If it was you who sent the first letter, and Shark that accepted, then Shark's terms apply.

This is what is called the 'battle of the forms'. It pays to watch it.

Selling and the law

Traditionally, the law of sale was quite simple: 'caveat emptor', or, let the buyer beware. The terms were whatever the two parties agreed. Put another way, the big fishes were allowed to eat the little fishes, and the Shark Supply approach was the winning approach. The small consumer was the loser.

The law has stepped in with a series of important laws: the Sales of Goods Acts and the Supply of Goods and Services Act, the Trades Descriptions Acts, the Fair Trading Act, the Consumer Protection Acts, the Weights and Measures Acts, the Consumer Safety Acts, the Consumer Credit Act – the list is long. Many of these Acts deal with all sales and supplies, whilst others cover only supplies to private consumers. Let's see what effect they have on Shark Supplies' terms.

Clause 2 (page 110) is a good example of the problems of handling small print. Part of it is rubbish. You only deal on Shark's terms if they form part of the acceptance by Shark of your offer, or you accept Shark's offer with these terms in it and without objecting. And then they only form part of the agreement if drawn to your attention. Here, Shark would say they were, because it said 'conditions (over)' on the front of the form. Merely signing the form is not important. The other part is a notice that limits the authority of all Shark staff to alter these terms, so if you reached a verbal agreement with a Shark salesman that altered one of the terms, Shark could say it was not authorised, and go back to their standard terms.

'your problem is our opportunity'

Shark Supplies

Unit 10, Waterway Estate,
Crabington, Bucks MK92 1Q2

Phone: 0654 321090 (Ansaphone)
Emergencies: 0901 234560

VAT No 0654 3210 98

All supplies on our standard terms and conditions (over)

INVOICE dated . . 30. Feb . . 1990

To supplying and fitting replacement placer widget on customer's premises, as per urgent order	300	
urgent order supplement	100	
parts	50	
delivery	50	500.00
Plus VAT at 15%		75
Due		£575.00

This pretend small print was designed to bring out two points. The first is to sort out when a **contract** is reached for a supply. The second is to emphasise the importance of the **laws governing sales**, especially consumer sales.

1 Did you remember to look at the small print on the back of the invoice. Most people don't. Which is, of course, why sellers and buyers alike both resort to it in order to stack the contract terms of the sale on the invoice as much in their own interests and against those of the other party to the contract as they can, whilst no one else is looking. The other purpose of the small print is to clear up all the legal doubts and unstated terms of the usual business contract. The rest of the small print on this page looks at issues that could have been hidden in the small print – along with those which the law imposes or forbids.

2 **Standard terms** The terms and conditions set out herein (called the 'standard terms') form part of the terms and conditions of the sale of goods and supply of services invoiced on this document. The buyer agrees to them by signing the document. The seller's servants and agents have no authority to alter them by any oral representation, and the terms can only be altered by express written alteration properly authorised by the seller.

3 **Quotations and estimates** The price payable by the buyer for goods and services supplied by the seller is that shown on this invoice notwithstanding any quotation or estimate or other sum quoted or estimated by the seller to the buyer. Any such quotation or estimate whilst being given in good faith is to be taken as a rough guide price only, exclusive of value added tax, and exclusive of the seller's standard additional charges for immediate and urgent work, for delivery, and any other additions by the seller. Any extra goods or services ordered by the customer are chargeable to the customer in full.

4 **Goods and services to be supplied** Whilst the seller will use its best endeavours to ensure that the goods supplied by it are fully to the buyer's specifications (or in the absence of specifications are of a reasonable quality for the work to be undertaken by the seller) and that the services supplied by the seller are of a reasonable quality the seller undertakes no warranty whatsoever as to the quality of goods and services supplied and the buyer is on notice to raise with the seller's appropriate representative before the supply of goods is accepted or before any supply of services is completed and for the purposes of this provision a supply of goods is treated as taking place when the goods are appropriated to the buyer's order whether or not they have been delivered to the buyer at that time and a supply of services is taken to be completed at the time stated by the seller's representatives to be the completion of the work. The Sale of Goods Act shall not apply to this contract.

5 **Terms of payment** Payment of this invoice is due seven days from the date thereof whether or not it has been delivered to the buyer within that time, and the seller shall have the right to charge interest at ten per cent above the basic lending rate of its banker as posted by that banker from time to time on any moneys outstanding from the date that payment on the invoice is due. Payment by instalments or retentions against work are not acceptable to the seller unless agreed in advance of the work being undertaken or the goods delivered.

6 **Seller's lien** The seller retains the title to all goods supplied until such time as the buyer has paid in full the sums owned to the seller as invoiced by the seller for goods and services supplied. In the event of non-payment of all charges so invoiced the seller reserves in full its rights to the property on all goods supplied including the right to enter upon the buyer's premises at any time of day or night to repossess the goods provided only that the seller in removing the goods shall not cause more damage to the buyer's premises and equipment than is reasonable in removing the goods as aforesaid.

7 **Delivery** Unless the seller and buyer agree otherwise before the conclusion of the contract for supply evidenced by this invoice the buyer shall be at risk in respect of all goods to be supplied from the time that they are unconditionally assigned to the buyer by the seller or at the seller's order. Whilst the seller will normally arrange for the delivery of goods the seller shall be entitled to charge the buyer for this delivery. Further the seller accepts no responsibility whatsoever for any delay occasioned in the delivery of goods or in the supply of services or any consequent damage that may be occasioned to the buyer or any other person by reason of the delay.

8 **Disputes** In the event of the buyer raising any issue under this contract or disputing in any way the correctness of the price, delivery, quality, quantity or any other aspect of the goods or services supplied under this contract the buyer shall not be permitted to take any action in the courts and the seller reserves the right to refer the matter in the absence of agreement to an arbitrator selected by the seller and the buyer shall bear the costs of all fees payable to the arbitrator in respect of such arbitration provided only that such charges shall be reasonable for the work undertaken on the seller's instructions.

9 **General** And if you thought these terms and conditions were splendid and just what you ought to put in your contract – don't, because you might well be committing a criminal offence, and even if it was not criminal several of these terms will not work in law.

Is the price right?

The clauses on quotes, payment and deliveries are quite important, but also a try-on. The price is – or should be – agreed when the contract is made. If a price has not been agreed, it is quite possible that there is no real agreement, and therefore no contract. Once it is fixed, or its basis is agreed, that cannot be changed. It's no good going back and saying a mistake was made, or that a standard charge not yet mentioned is 'always added' to bills. For the same reason, if you do not mention VAT, and then add it on, the customer would be fully entitled to refuse to pay. If VAT is not mentioned, it is assumed to be included in the price. Further, under the new Consumer Protection Act it will be an offence to give any consumer a misleading indication of goods, service, accommodation or facilities. Shark might fall foul of that, as well as the Trades Descriptions Acts.

The quality must be right

The clause on the quality of goods and services is also illegal. All contracts to consumers, whether formal, or over the counter sales, must contain these terms:

- Goods must **correspond with their description**. If they don't, consumers must be entitled to a refund, or to goods that do match the description, and possibly to compensation.
- Goods sold by sample must **match the sample**. Again, if they don't, the customer can demand his money back.
- Goods must be **fit for the purpose** for which they are supplied so if Shark was asked for parts for a particular purpose, they must work for that purpose.
- Goods sold by description must be of **merchantable quality**, unless the seller has pointed out defects to the

buyer, the buyer has inspected or has been given a chance to inspect. This means, in effect, they must be reasonable value for the price paid. Sale goods, even if there is no inspection, will not be expected to be as good as full price goods.

These terms apply, whatever the contract says. And it is an offence to try, as Shark does, to get out of them. If you want further guidance, get in touch with your local council's **Trading Standards officers**, whose job it is to supervise these laws, and who are as ready to advise retailers as consumers.

The buyer's remedies

The clause trying to remove the buyer's right to a remedy also will not work. But the law is confusing. For example, the following is illegal:

NO REFUNDS MADE AFTER PURCHASE

while there is nothing wrong with this:

NO GOODS EXCHANGED AFTER PURCHASE

Why? Because a seller is never required to exchange goods, faulty or not. His obligation in law is to refund money if the goods are not what is ordered under the contract, and the buyer returns the goods for that reason within a reasonable time, or to pay damages (or compensation) if the goods fall short of the required standard and the buyer chooses to keep them. Attempting to avoid a customer's right to a refund in appropriate cases is illegal. Refusing to exchange goods – even faulty goods – is not. The law may be way out of line with what most people want but you must observe it.

Use proper standard conditions

Though the law deals with all those points, it does not deal, for instance, with delivery nor the seller's lien (which Shark is not alone in claiming). A proper contract should cover all these points and, in a more sensible way than Shark, it may cover arbitration too. Many trade associations (for example, travel agents and removers) have standard conditions worked out for the association. Some businesses have standard agreed forms of contract (especially in building and engineering). Get hold of these, and check if they are appropriate. Especially if you are in an unusual business, or there are higher than usual risks of disputes, get a lawyer to assess the problems and advise you on any standard conditions.

11 Raising cash

How much money is needed to get started? Where do you get it? We will take the questions in that order, as it is almost as dangerous to raise too much cash as too little.

How much money?

There are two parts to this – a budget of how much start-up money is needed, and a cash-flow forecast of how fast cash will go through the business. A business can founder if it gets either of these wrong, even though it is basically profitable, so we need to be careful.

A start-up budget

Whether you are buying a business, buying into a franchise, or starting from scratch, you need funds to get started – to buy capital items (the premium on a lease, or new equipment) and to cover running costs and your personal expenses until the business becomes profitable. Much of this money is needed up-front, with further injections of new money from time to time as things develop.

Opposite is a checklist of items your start-up budget should cover.

Checklist: Start-up costs

Premises

- capital cost of buying; or premium and rent in advance ... £
- legal and survey fees .... £
- repair and maintenance, and service charge in advance .... £
- rates due at start .... £
- adaption of premises, eg new shop front, telephones .... £

Plant and machinery

- purchase of equipment, or first payments under leases .... £
- cost of moving, installing, adapting equipment .... £
- purchase of car or van .... £
- initial running expenses .... £

Stock

- purchase of initial stock for resale, supply .... £
- initial stocks of other consumables, eg leaflets .... £

Goodwill

- if buying a business or franchise, the price .... £

Staffing

- initial wages, commissions, professional fees .... £
- your personal expenses for initial period .... £

Other

- initial interest payments and finance costs .... £
- contingency reserve (to cover what you didn't think about) .... £

TOTAL (for . . . months) .... £

Have you noticed two variables in this checklist? The first is that some items can be obtained in different ways – buying or renting premises or equipment; getting cash or credit for stock. The second is that the timescale can be altered – when do you need cash for personal expenses, and for how long?

To tackle the timescale, we need another kind of checklist, a cash flow forecast, as we saw in Chapter 6, 'Plan it'.

The business should now have three financial plans (or best guesses): the cash flow forecast, the profit forecast and income budget, and the start-up budget. Armed with these, we can see where to start the cash flowing.

Raising the cash

You have two sources of capital: your own, and money granted by or borrowed from others. The relationship between these is regarded as highly significant by professional lenders, and is given a fancy name, **gearing**. The gearing of a business is the ratio:

borrowed capital: own capital

A business is said to be **highly geared** if borrowing is high compared with owner's capital, and low if the reverse holds. Lenders start worrying when a small business is geared more than 1:1, ie loans exceed assets owned outright, and therefore what the business is worth, so the level of risk is high.

Lenders are concerned to see how much capital the owner is investing. Anyway, why should they put their money at risk if you will not? The other point of which they are well aware is that if you invest up to the hilt in your business, you are going to work your hardest to make sure it succeeds. So, the first source of finance must always be **you**.

What are you worth?

Probably more than you think. Those who have been made redundant, or have retired will have some funds available. Do you own your own home? Most of us do. What is it worth? That will depend on where you live. So also will decisions on whether it is wise to sell the house and look for somewhere else cheaper in order to free some cash and, perhaps, cut down on living expenses for the time being. It's crazy, but in some parts of the country, the house may go up in value more than any business you run from the cash realised on a sale, whilst in other areas houses are actually going down in value, and loss-cutting could make a lot of sense. There are no easy rules.

If you don't sell, you may still use your house as security for a mortgage or additional mortgage, as this is usually one of the best sources of borrowed money. Don't forget though, that the rest of the family are also living there, so it's their home that's at risk, too. This is something about which you should be completely honest with the family right from the start. When your business proves to be a success they will enjoy their share of the benefits too. But if things do go wrong, perhaps for an unforeseen reason, they will also be at risk.

What about your other savings and investments? These should certainly be used, rather than borrowing expensively elsewhere, and to keep the gearing in your favour. You may have small shareholdings and other lump sum investments that you can cash in to advantage (and it's usually going to be better for you to invest in your own business rather than investing in other people's). You may have life policies or pension plans that can be used as a way of raising cash – your insurance company will be able to tell you whether or not you can arrange a loan alongside them. This is often a better long-term solution than cashing your life assurance in. In the first place it has a low value in the early years (as it is designed more for protection than savings) and in the second place, what might seem a good decision now could be regretted bitterly in 20 years time.

Help from the family

Similarly, think through your other assets. Does the family need two cars? Do you know how much a car costs to run each year? My (ordinary Austin) car cost £36 a week last year, whilst my wife's bang-about Mini cost another £15 a week. Come to that, do you know what your family budget is? How will that fit in with your plans? If you don't know, then your budgeting ought to start *today*, so get that pencil out!

Use the start of your business as the start of your personal economies, not the end of them. It is very tempting to use an expense account or the tax advantages available to get a bigger car. It may seem to have advantages in giving you the right image for your new business – or so any competent car salesman will tell you. But if it bleeds you of badly-needed cash, it will not be long before others are driving the car, and you are at the bus stop.

The family may also help with loans on easy terms – easy, that is, until Uncle Egbert is unexpectedly made redundant and needs his money back urgently. If you borrow that way, it is only fair to realise that they may need the capital more than you at a time when it is not easy for you to repay. Be as businesslike with family loans as with strangers'.

Raising cash from others

This can be done by getting others to join in your business, or buy a stake in it, or by grants or commercial loans. You can get others involved in the business, and putting up their own capital, in a number of ways:

- by bringing them in as **partners**, perhaps as **sleeping partners**
- by forming a **company**, and selling them some of the shares
- by setting up as a **cooperative**.

The price in each case is that the business is theirs as well as yours. The pros and cons have been discussed in Chapter 5, 'Two's a company'.

Grants

There are people prepared to give you money to help your new business get going, if it's the right sort of business in the right place. One of them is me – in my official capacity as one of Her Majesty's payers of tax. There are also business charities willing to help. Why? Enterprise is a good thing, especially in areas of high unemployment.

We looked at various sources in Chapter 4, 'Get the experts in'. Look again. There may be help for you which will make quite a difference to your cash projections. In particular, check out the **Enterprise Allowance**, if you have not yet done so. That would alter your income by £40 a week, just to start. Also, read again the section on the Prince's Youth Business Trust to see how it provides cash to new businesses.

Borrowing from the bank

The primary sources of money for the small business are the High Street **banks**, all of which have small business units. They can offer help by way of **overdraft** or **fixed term loans**. The cheapest and most flexible method is an overdraft. This means that you can draw up to an agreed amount more out of your bank account than you have in it. You pay interest for this, but on a daily basis and at up to 4% more than the bank's base rate. The idea is that you only pay on what you have borrowed that day. Technically, an overdraft is repayable to the bank on demand, but if things are not going badly the bank will probably review the overdraft with you each year or so.

Fixed interest loans usually cost more, and tie you down more, but are necessary to raise larger amounts of cash. There is plenty of scope for choice at the beginning – the length of the loan, whether there is a **repayment holiday** (a period during which no repayments have to be made) at the beginning of the loan, and so on. But once started, the agreed repayments must be met. And it can prove very expensive to pay such loans off early.

Plan your borrowing so that you borrow enough (including a margin for error) but aim to pay it back as soon as practicable – perhaps over a three year term, unless you can see good profit reasons why longer term loans are necessary.

Lenders like **security** behind a loan. With a company, directors will be asked for personal guarantees. Lenders often also want to see life assurance policies to make sure they get their money back if anything happens to the borrower. They may ask for a mortgage of the owner's or director's house or other assets. But there is help here for you with the Government's **Loan Guarantee Scheme.** The Government will guarantee up to 70% of your loan, in exchange for a premium from you of £25 for each £1000 borrowed. Ask the bank manager for details.

Besides the banks, others may be prepared to put money up as loans on a commercial basis, for example **insurance companies,** and also **Investment in Industry** (3 i), a company set up by the Bank of England and the major banks specifically to lend money to business. These may be much more interested in larger loans than the clearing banks, and if you are confidently thinking big, they may be able to help you think even bigger. The other bodies set up to help small businesses, such as **CoSIRA** (see Chapter 4, 'Get in the experts') also have access to funds, sometimes at cheap rates of interest, or are able to give grants towards the cost of interest on loans.

To find out about what is available in grants and loans, do not forget to ask your local enterprise agency for help. They will know what's available locally, and may well be able to help with introductions. And check with the bank manager whether he knows of other sources.

Be prepared

Don't scout around for loans in a haphazard way. The bank manager will be pleased to see you – if you approach getting the loan in a businesslike way. Do it with the professional attitude to your business you intend to adopt when you get going. Make an appointment, and go armed with some impressive details.

Most important, lenders want to see plans and cash projections. They want to know about your start-up budget, your cash flow projections, your profit and loss budget, and your business plans. If you have not set your pencil to work on these, they will not be very impressed. If you have, they will quite probably help with advice on improving them, as well as coming up with the money, if the figures are right.

A final word. Beware of money that is too easy to come by, and always check what is the true cost of the loan. Lenders are obliged by law to show you this, as well as a standard form of interest rate – the **APR** or annual percentage rate. Watch for other charges besides the interest, for example setting-up or introduction fees, professional charges and settlement fees at the end. These can add substantially to the total cost of the loan. Watch also that if you borrow through a broker, you can end up paying even more. The **broker's**

fee will not be included in the APR. What is more, because what may happen is that the fee is added to the amount of loan borrowed, then 'disappears' when granted to leave you with the amount you originally wanted, you will end up paying interest on the charge throughout the period of the loan. That can prove costly.

Buying on credit

An alternative means of financing the purchase of cars or equipment is through credit sales or hire purchase. At best these are extremely good ways of buying, but at worst very pricey. I say 'at best' because offers of interest-free credit sales do occur from time to time, allowing you to phase payment over perhaps ten months on cars and some goods. In other cases the APR may be 30% or more, and much more expensive than borrowing through your bank or on a fixed term loan.

When starting, you may find suppliers will make stock available to you on credit terms or on special sale or return terms, and they may perhaps share in special offers with you which cut the cost to you of initial purchases. Franchisors should normally be expected to help their franchisees at the beginning.

Other forms of finance are more readily available for the expanding business and are discussed in Chapter 16, 'Growing bigger'.

12 Control your money

Let me introduce you to the black (or secret) economy. It is frequented by those who keep no books or records of what they do, never charge VAT or pay NI contributions or income tax. You don't need the introduction, I'm sure. Their approach is disarmingly, if dispiritingly, simple. Its cheaper for them and cheaper for you. If they charge you £50, they pocket it. To pocket £50 after income tax, NI and VAT would mean a bill of about £80.

Who needs accounts?

If this tempts you, I could tell you the penalties the tax authorities and the courts impose on such people when they catch them (which they do quite often). But that's not the real reason for keeping things straight. Rather, it is because you need to control your money so that your business grows properly. Those in the 'black' economy are often actually in the red. They have no pension to retire on, or sickness benefit if they are ill, and probably no savings. And they may have no idea whether they are working for a profit or for nothing.

Without good records, you will flounder. You will not know how much profit you are making, and will probably lose track of bills people owe you (though they won't lose track of your debts). You will not be using the money invested in your business as best you could.

What accounts should I keep?

Companies are required to produce accounts annually in a set form, and must keep proper records to satisfy the auditors that the accounts are right. Partnerships need to keep proper books to satisfy all the partners that they are getting the right share of the profits. A sole trader can keep records in any form he or she likes and these will not need auditing. To give an idea of what a year's accounts should show, some simplified accounts in audited form are included, following the format imposed on small companies. Wibble Widgets Ltd is a £100 company, that is, it has 100 £1 shares, 99 of which belong to its director/owner Mr Wibble.

ACCOUNTS OF WIBBLE WIDGETS LTD

Year ending 31 March 19 . .

Profit and loss account for the year ending 31 March 19 . .

Turnover (sales):			50000
Cost of sales: (a)			
Opening stock		4500	
Purchases		15000	
Delivery costs		500	
Wages		15000	
		35000	
Less closing stock		5000	
			30000
Gross profit			20000
Rental income			1000
			21000
Less Rent and service charge		2500	
Rates		800	
Heat and light		400	
Telephone		300	
Repairs		500	
Publicity		200	
Stationery and post		100	
Van expenses		1000	
Insurance		300	
Interest		500	
Bank charges		100	
Legal and audit fees		200	
Sundries		100	
Depreciation		500	7500
Net profit before tax			13500
Tax			1500
Net profit for the year			**12000**

Notes
(a) the cost of goods sold includes all direct costs of selling the goods.
Sometimes this includes wage costs, sometimes not – it is one of the many
variable items in accounts. To leave out wage costs here will sharply increase
the gross profit, but make no difference to the net profit.
(b) any unusual features ought to be the subject of notes to the accounts.

The law also requires some other points (left out here for simplicity) to
be covered in notes.

Balance sheet as at 31 March 19 . .

ASSETS

Fixed assets:	
Land and buildings	6000
Plant and machinery	3000
Fixtures and fittings	1000
Current assets:	
Stock	5000
Debtors	4000
Total	19000

LIABILITIES

Capital and reserves:	
Share capital paid up	100
Reserves (a)	7900
Creditors:	
Long-term bank loan (b)	5000
Hire purchase	2000
Trade creditors	1000
Bank overdraft	1000
Taxation	1500
Loan to director	500
Total	19000

Notes
(a) The reserves include the balance of value of the assets over the other liabilities, as it is the general balance of value of the business. It will equal the reserves of the business at the end of the previous year, plus/minus any changes in the values of the assets plus the net profit for the current year, less the amount of those profits already paid to the owners. The figures indicate that Wibble has already had most of the £12000 profit.
(b) This is a long term liability, but the other creditors are all current liabilities as they are repayable at short notice.

The law requires other details, left out here for simplicity.

AUDITORS' REPORT TO THE MEMBERS OF WIBBLE WIDGETS LTD
We have audited the above financial statements in accordance with approved Auditing Standards. In our opinion these statements, which were prepared under the historical cost convention, give a true and fair view of the state

of the company as at 31 March 19 . . and its profits for the year ended then and comply with the Companies Act 1985.   *Audit Ors & Co*

The profit and loss account shows the profit (or loss) of the business for a stated period (usually a year). It does so in two stages. First, the gross profit (or direct profit from sales) is shown by taking the direct cost of sales from the sales receipts, taking account of the amount of stock held at both ends of the period. Then the other administrative costs and overheads are deducted to produce a net profit – the 'bottom line' we so often hear of. Accounts can show us much more than just the profit. Turn back to Chapter 3, 'Buying a business' and try the tests there.

Balance sheets are not accounts. They are a sort of 'freeze frame' view of the company on one day – the last of the financial year. They tell us what the business is worth, and how strong it is on that day. A better view can be gained by comparing that picture with those of previous years – again using the tests we saw in 'Buying a business'. What you are doing is using these accounts as management accounts.

The accounts and balance sheet of a little business like this, whilst telling a lot, can also alter a lot, just as can the accounts of any business. For example, wages could have been put as a deduction against gross profits, rather than a figure in finding gross profits. What's the difference? The effect is a decrease in gross profits, but a reduction in the general overheads of the business.

On a balance sheet we do not know how the various items amongst the assets are valued. How are the (leased) premises worth £6,000, or the van and other equipment £3,000? If the values were to be increased or decreased, the effect would also be to increase or decrease the capital reserves by the same amount, as that is the figure which makes the accounts balance.

Keeping the books

To keep records necessary to produce accounts and a balance sheet like these – and to satisfy the auditors Wibble is not inventing the whole thing – Wibble Widgets Ltd needed a full bookkeeping system. What do you need?

The records needed will vary depending on your business. A retailer with a limited range of products sold for cash only can get by with the daily till total and a weekly list of expenses, totalling costs and sales up over the year in a simple accounts book, such as those made by Collins. So can a jobbing serviceman who gives out bills, and collects in the cash, for each job as he goes along. But the moment sales are for credit, things need tightening (see Chapter 13, 'Controlling their cash' next). And if the owner wants to get some idea of which his best lines are, and how much profit different items make, fuller records are needed. It is wise to design the records so errors can be checked.

Patented systems requiring double entries (as a fail-safe) such as those sold by Kalamazoo have long been available. The up to date equivalent is a simple computer based system (see Chapter 16, 'Growing bigger'), but exercise books will serve if kept properly. In whatever form, you need:

- a cash book in which to record all payments and receipts (or total takings)
- a petty cash book or vouchers to avoid cluttering up the cash book with every packet of biscuits or pencil you buy
- customer accounts (or sales accounts) for all credit sales
- purchase accounts if you want to keep track separately of different kinds of expense, and to check on the bills you owe each supplier

and, if you want to keep part of the records confidential,
- a private account to handle partners' or directors' money.

It is part of an auditor's job to tell you if the books and

records are adequate for proper accounting for the business. Even if your business does not need auditing, by far the best people to advise on bookkeeping are accountants. Ask yours for advice before you make their job harder (and pricier) than it need be.

The cash book

This is the heart of the system. It is where you record all business receipts and payments except minor payments noted by a petty cash system. It should record every sum coming into or leaving the business, along with its date, and from whom or to whom it is transferred. In time-honoured conventions, a cash book looks like this:

Receipts				Payments			
date	details	ref	£	date	details	ref	£
29/2	Wangle Widgets	CW1	100 00	29/2	Post Office		16 00
				29/2	Wobble Widgets SW2		62 00

Receipts always go on the left, and payments go on the right. The 'ref' column allows you to insert a reference across to another account, eg a receipt from Wangle Widgets also goes into a customer account CW1.

A petty cash book (or vouchers you can buy in a stationers) keeps track of the little things every business needs to buy. The simplest way is the little tin box with a cash 'float' replaced by vouchers as it is spent. Each time the float is topped up, the payment is recorded in the cash book.

Sales and purchases accounts

We use the same format to produce accounts to keep track of transfers between the business and each customer and supplier (or kind of overhead).

That will look something similar:

SALES ACCOUNT—Account No: CWI... Customer.........								
29/1	Invoice 602	100	00	29/2	CB	Cheque	100	00

When we supply Wangle Widgets, we enter it into account CW1 on the right hand side (we have paid them in kind). When they pay, it goes on the left as a receipt, cancelling out the other side. At the same time it goes into the cash book as a receipt, showing we now have the money.

Of course, these can be books, cards, a computer programme, forms – even backs of envelopes as long as we don't lose them.

Bank accounts

Your bank will also be keeping a parallel set of accounts of all your payments into and out of your bank accounts. These need cross-checking with your own accounts, perhaps every month. Do that for two reasons. The first is to spot any errors made by the bank or any frauds on you and the bank. Secondly, the bank's version of your accounts provides a useful way of spotting your own errors.

To check both the bank's accounts and your own, you should receive monthly statements from the bank, and reconcile them with your own accounts. If there are no errors, the balance on the bank statement should be reconciled with the closing balance for the month in your cash book, following this formula:

	Closing bank balance
plus	items not credited
less	cheques unpresented
equals	Closing cash book balance

The **items not credited** are items which have appeared as receipts in your cash book, but have not yet been credited to your bank account (perhaps they have not been paid in). The **cheques unpresented** are those payments out which you have sent, and therefore written into the cash book as paid out, but which have not yet been presented for payment to your bank. As a cheque takes several days to get back to your bank if sent by post, there will normally be some cheques outstanding at the end of any month. If the two totals do not reconcile, start hunting for errors.

Managing with figures

Once you have decent accounts, you can see what you're doing. Your budget (see Chapter 6, 'Plan it') will start to make sense – or nonsense, in which case you can take action. You can monitor your cash flow (see Chapter 11, 'Raising cash'), and act before you hit the rocks. And you can start to control other people's cash which ought to be yours.

13 Controlling their cash

Giving credit to customers cannot usually be avoided, but it is risky, costly, ties up funds and should be strictly controlled. Granting credit on any scale is also a tightly regulated business. You must therefore monitor all business credit fully from the start.

Manage credit

However your customers are granted credit, it is your money involved. It is at risk until you receive it, and cannot be used until then. Further, letting money stand out can be expensive, unless customers are paying properly for the privilege.

Do you need to let customers have credit except for short periods, or at all? Could you insist your customers pay weekly rather than monthly? Could you allow a discount for those who pay promptly? In reality, they pay the proper price. Those who do not get the discount are paying also for the money you are lending them.

Do you pay – and have to pay – more promptly than your customers? If anything, you should aim to err the other way. The trouble is – everyone else is trying that game too. And, in the nature of things, bigger firms get away with it more than smaller businesses. A statement of best practice, **Payment on time** (obtainable from the Small Firms Service) is aimed to encourage prompt payment, and stop businesses being cash-starved by late bills.

Speed up customer payment

Do your customers pay in advance? They should, if you are paying out money for them in advance too. Get a deposit, or an advance for buying materials whenever possible. Ask for deposits against work done. That cuts your credit problem. At the same time, it gives you protection against customers who want to change their minds. What about budget accounts, savings clubs and similar schemes? You may need to induce customers to use these by special offers, but it can be worth it.

Unintended credit

Do not neglect incidental credit. If a customer pays by cheque or credit card, how much **delay** is there before you pay it into a bank? Do you pay in daily, or once a week? The whole time you are holding the cheque, your customer is benefiting.

The main source of unintended credit is **inefficiency in billing**. If it takes you a month to make up a bill which then allows four further weeks to pay, that's two months free credit already. If you do not chase the account promptly, and the customer grudgingly then pays by cheque, another month or more may have gone. All the time you are paying for that cash – or your best and promptest customers are. If you have many customers like that, you will be permanently extending thousands of pounds in unnecessary trade credit, which you cannot use and for which you are paid nothing.

What steps are you taking to deal with **aged debts**, those that have been unpaid for some time? Separate lists of those bills left unpaid for, say, 30 and 60 days will make sure you devote more time to getting them paid, and are aware of who the slow payers are. Computer-based accounts systems can do that sort of thing automatically. Any other system needs a human equivalent, perhaps a monthly check of all customer accounts.

Retentions

When you finish a job, is it really finished? The sloppy practice of many small businesses under time pressure is to finish enough of the work to get the customer off your back, and then rush off to the next job, leaving the last bits unfinished. Finding time for those last bits can then be a problem. So, a little embarrassed, you don't send out the bill. Or, more brazenly, you do send the bill, but the customer only pays part of it. If sensible, the customer will keep back quite a bit more than the outstanding work will cost. Your problem is that, if you leave too many ends untied like this, you will run out of cash, as well as create a lot of dissatisfied customers.

Reduce the risks

Take steps to ensure your customers' debts become bad debts as seldom as possible. A bad debt is one you cannot get paid. Not only are you losing the use of that money, you may never get it. Further, the tax charge on your business is probably based on what you have earned, not what you have received. You may have paid tax on a bad debt before your customer pays it. Only when it becomes clear that your customer will not pay at all will you get tax relief.

Set up a procedure for checking properly whenever you are

paid by cheque or a credit card, that they are properly filled in and appear valid. Make sure customers produce a **cheque guarantee card** to back their cheques, and that they are not out of date. Be wary of accepting a company cheque from an unknown customer unless there is, again, some way of confirming it. Many garages, from bitter experience, simply refuse to accept company cheques. Customers can usually pay some other way, if they can pay at all.

There are, of course, more ways than one of checking a customer. Last year, I bought a car in a small garage, and was utterly amazed when firstly it was reserved for me without a deposit, and then I was allowed to drive it away having paid by a cheque which was not cleared or checked in any way. Afterwards, it dawned on me that in chatting whilst we tried the car, they had checked our family's credentials locally, and my cheque was taken because they were known. Even so, that assumes I was who I said I was, and that was not checked.

All the garage needed to do was to pick up the telephone and ask the bank whether I was good for the amount of my cheque. Had I been a fraudster, I would probably have disappeared quietly. The garage could also have had my cheque **specially cleared** before I was allowed to collect the vehicle. That costs a pound or two, but means prompt payment and early use of the money with the risk gone. As it was, we drove the car around for a week before our bank paid up for us.

Credit cards are a two-edged blessing. You get the guarantee, but you have to pay a discount for it. And you're not always paid promptly by the charge card company. However, some customers (like me) carry as little cash as possible, so won't buy if you only accept cash. And they are increasingly used by businesses to tighten up on the way spending of staff is checked.

Take precautions when lending

Check the identity and credit-worthiness of any large credit customer. The following suggestions will help:

- Is he who he says he is? Check banker's cards, driving licences or other evidence of identity, preferably something with a signature or photograph attached. Keep a note of the details of what you checked.
- Build in a delay between getting the agreement and delivering the goods, to allow checks to be made.
- Ask for references. Inquire where the customer banks, and ask your own bank for a **banker's reference** from the customer's bank. The reply will be guarded, but useful. Take up trade references. Do not just think how impressive the reference sounds, and be scared off. You might be calling a bluff.
- If you suspect the customer is **bankrupt**, check by searching the official bankruptcy register maintained by the Land Charges Registry. You can get the special forms from any law stationer. If you suspect the customer has other bad debts, check with the local county court **register of judgment debts**, which lists all debts confirmed as due by the court.
- In appropriate cases, employ a **credit reference agency** to check your customer's credit rating. This will check official sources, including also lists of those with hire purchase debts, and probably keep large files of its own.
- If the customer is a **company**, get the files at the Companies Registration Office checked. You can do this cheaply and quickly by a **company search**, which can be used to find out how big the company is, who the directors are, what its address is, and so forth. When dealing with companies, watch the **ultra vires** point dealt with in Chapter 5, 'Two's a company'. If you deal with a company with which you have no connection in good faith, then the law will protect you, but it will not enforce a company contract where you are on notice that the

company has no power under its objects to undertake that contract.

- Get **security** for your loan – big business does. If dealing with a company, get a guarantee from the directors. If dealing with a young person for the first time, get a security deposit or a personal guarantee from someone else (the gas and electricity people do just this). Or make sure you protect your **seller's lien** (the right of an unpaid seller to hold the goods), or **reserve the title** in the goods until you are paid, by using properly drawn up standard conditions (see Chapter 10, 'Big sales, small print' and get legal advice).
- Make it clear you **get tough** on defaulting debtors. Check out the best way of getting a debt enforced, and let it be known that you will use that route.

Enforcing payment

Sooner or later, someone will default on you. Take proper precautions to reduce and check credit, and it will be later. When it happens, you need a procedure to deal with it. Start with an **aged debtors procedure**. Send a clear reminder after, say, 30 days, and a stronger one after another 15 or 30. After that, you could telephone to find out why payment is not made, having first decided what you regard as a plausible excuse, if any! At this point, check any contract you have. Are you entitled to seize the goods back, or demand an arbitration?

If all else fails to get the bill paid, either take firm action, or write the bill off there and then. It should be said immediately that taking court action may not be worthwhile to cover a smaller bill if you get your solicitor to do it. And by 'smaller' I mean less than about £200. You can collect these yourself through the county court's **Small Claims** procedure. Your local county court has a booklet on *Small Claims* which explains it, and the court clerks will also help.

Even a solicitor's letter costs money. But a firm letter threatening proceedings in a formal manner, and giving a short period of seven to 14 days addressed to a senior member of the business gets a lot of bills paid. After that, court proceedings are your only course of action. Two final points on this. Court proceedings are slow. Also, there is no guarantee that the judgment you obtain will be paid. If the debtor is unemployed, or has no assets you are wasting your time. That should also be checked if possible first.

Bankruptcy and liquidation

When a business runs out of money, there is usually something left. This goes first to any secured creditors – that is, those with mortgages, seller's liens, and similar arrangements. Next come the employees and the Government (to collect taxes outstanding). Only then come the ordinary trade creditors. In many cases there will be some money for them, but not much. In such cases, the liquidator pays a 'dividend' to each of the creditors who has registered as being owed money by the bankrupt. It is only part payment, but make sure you register any claim. And at that point you may get some tax relief.

Making a debtor bankrupt is the very last resort of a creditor. It is expensive and, for the reasons just shown, does not always work. But it is an extremely powerful threat as it may result in the debtor losing home and possibly job, plus any bank accounts, savings and most other assets. Get legal advice before you take such a drastic and expensive step.

Consumer credit licences

Anyone lending money to consumers as part of their business, or advising on credit, needs to have a consumer credit licence. There are various kinds of licence depending on what you are doing. The Office of Fair Trading publishes a series of booklets about this. Your Small Firms Service or local enterprise agency should be able to help you get some – but make enquiries at the start if your business involves the grant of, or advice about, credit (other than the ordinary credit where customers are given a short period to pay).

14 Your share – their share

Unless you want to be a 'ghost' you must plan to share the profits from your business and to save from them for your own and your family's future. A 'ghost', in tax jargon, is someone who for official purposes does not exist and never pays taxes. Unless your profits are too low, you will be paying tax. You should also be planning to ensure you can afford to retire in due course, and provide your family with some security if anything happens to you. As the taxman helps pay for private pensions and some savings, whilst also collecting contributions for state pensions, the two topics can be looked at together.

These are both topics of considerable detail and importance. Because of that, I have written a companion book to this one, **Tax for the Self-Employed**. It covers social security as well as all the taxes that affect you. In addition, Tony Reardon has written **Planning Your Pension** about the extremely important new pensions rules that came into effect in 1988 and 1989, also in this series. Here, therefore, we only deal with the key points you need to know at the start.

You and the taxman

When you decide to launch your business, notify:

- the **Inland Revenue**, who collect income and corporation taxes from your business and anyone you employ;
- the **VAT Office** of Customs and Excise if you need to

register for VAT (which you must do if your sales are high enough);
- the **DSS**, through your local **Social Security Office**, to deal with your NI contributions and benefit entitlement, and those of anyone you employ.

How do you do this, and when?

Telling the Revenue

You must advise the Revenue that you have started business on your own account (or about your company, if there is a new one) by the end of the first year of business. The best way of doing this is to ask the office of the local H M Inspector of Taxes (see under Inland Revenue in the phone book) for booklet **IR 28, Starting in Business**. This has a form at the back, **41G**, to be sent in to the local tax office. (There is also a copy in Tax for the Self-Employed.) It covers all the tax issues that need sorting out. The Revenue publish some other useful leaflets as well. Get: **IR53, Thinking of taking someone on? PAYE for employers** and **IR57, Thinking of working for yourself?**, also **CGT11, Capital Gains Tax and the Small Businessman**, to learn something of another tax you need to be aware of.

Three things covered by form 41G need checking from the start. First, are you appointing accountants (if your business is a company, you must)? If so, it may be best for them also to handle your **tax compliance** work (as accountants call sorting accounts out with the Revenue). Good accountants will more than pay back their fees doing this!

Second, choose the date to which you make up your first set of accounts carefully. You can save money by doing so if you are a sole trader or a partnership. This is because you pay tax on the profits for a year covered by your accounts in the next tax year after the date the accounts close. Whether your accounts end on 30 April 1990 or 31 March 1991, you will pay the tax due on the same dates (as the tax year starts on

6 April each year). An end-April accounts year means you keep the tax for almost a year longer. Again, if you have accountants, check with them.

Finally, if you are employing anyone whom you are paying more than about £45 a week (the figure varies from year to year), you must tell the Revenue. You are required to collect income tax from employees under the **PAYE** (Pay As You Earn) system. So accept my congratulations now. If you go into business, you will swiftly be appointed as one of H M Collectors of Taxes (honorary of course). And don't think you can get out of it by not telling them. If you should have collected the tax, and did not do so, *you* owe the tax, not the employee.

When you employ someone he should bring with him Form P45 on which is his code number and also the amount of tax paid so far that year. You will need to calculate PAYE according to various tax tables (ABC and D) and at the end of the financial year you will need to make a return (P14) of all income tax collected and National Insurance Contributions and finally hand to the employee a certificate (P60).

As well as collecting tax for the Inland Revenue you must also collect your employee's National Insurance contributions every week. There are many leaflets available from your local DSS office to help you with this task but NP15 Employer's Guide to National Insurance Contributions and NI208 National Insurance Contribution Rates will probably be the most helpful.

If you intend to be a labour only sub-contractor in the **construction industry**, you need a tax certificate before you can get paid by your main contractors without losing tax on the payment. Get leaflet **IR14, Tax deductions scheme explanatory booklet** to find out more.

Registering for VAT

Value Added Tax is exactly what it says. It is a tax (currently at the rate of 15%) on the value you add to goods which you have bought in at the time you are selling them. You calculate VAT by subtracting 15% of your raw material costs from the 15% tax charged on the goods that you sold. The difference between one lot of VAT and the other is the net VAT amount which you must pay to the Customs and Excise.

If your total turnover of VATable items in the last year was greater than £25,400 (or if, at any time, they will be greater than £25,400 in the next 30 days), register **for VAT** with the local VAT Office (address in the phone book). What are VATable items? Any item which is not **exempt** – nearly all goods for sale, and many kinds of services other than financial or welfare services. There is a full list in **Customs Notice VAT 700, The VAT guide**. Get a copy. The VAT Offices publish a series of leaflets about VAT. You should also get **Should I be registered for VAT?** and, if you are a retailer, **Customs Notice 727, Retail Schemes**. You register by filling in form **VAT 1** available from all VAT Offices.

You *must* register for VAT within 30 days of realising that your profits will exceed the limits in the next year, or have done so in the last three months or year. You have to pay VAT anyway, even if you don't register, and are also liable for penalties for not registering. Either get your accountants on to this, or get in touch with the VAT Office in good time.

VAT bookkeeping has been simplified for small businesses by two special procedures. First, any business with a turnover of under £250,000, and which meets other conditions, can elect to prepare VAT accounts on a cash basis, that is, by reference to money actually received and paid, not invoices. Second, these businesses can also apply to prepare annual accounts after the first year of registration, paying tax as an estimate.

Letting the DSS know

If you are going to be self-employed, inform your local Social Security Office (address in phone book). Also tell them if you are going to employ anyone earning over about £45 in any week from you. You have to collect NI contributions from those employees under the PAYE scheme, as well as paying contributions yourself on their earnings. You also need to sort out your own contribution liability.

To find out about this, and get the relevant forms, get the following leaflets from your local Social Security Office: **NI22, Stamping and Returning contribution cards for those paying Class 2 and Class 3 contributions, NI27A, People with small earnings from self-employment, NI41, NI guidance for the self-employed, NI 255, Class 2 and Class 3 contributions – the easy way to pay!, NP15, Employers guide to NI contributions, NP18, Class 4 contributions.** By way of translation, Class 1 contributions are those paid by employees and their employers, Class 2 is the flat-rate self-employed contribution, Class 4 is the earnings-related self-employed contribution (in effect extra income tax), and Class 3 are voluntary contributions for those not in employment.

If you have employees paying NI contributions, you are also responsible for paying any **statutory sick pay** or **statutory maternity pay** due to them. Get: **NI227, Employers guide to statutory sick pay** and **NI257, Employers guide to statutory maternity pay**, to find out more.

How to save tax

It is worth paying attention to tax rules, because you can easily pay more tax than needed, or even than the Government intends. That we cover in Tax for the Self-Employed, but one or two examples below, also show you how to do this. If Husband is self-employed and Wife is not at work, H should pay W for helping in the business weekly amounts up to just less than the lower figure for NI contributions (up to £46.00 a week in 1990). Below that W has to pay no NI contributions and (if she has no other earned income) no income tax, and H pays no NI contributions as her employer. If H wants to pay W more, he can do it in the form of non-taxable benefits in kind, or as pension contributions.

H employs part-time staff. One, E, earns about £80 a week. If E earns £80 a week, E and H both have to pay NI contributions (E pays £3.06, H pays £5.60), so E gets £76.94, and H pays £85.60. E also pays tax at 25% on each £1 over about £57 a week. If H paid E £77 and gave E free meals, costing £1 a day, H would still only pay £80.85 (because contributions on sums under £80 are at 5%). E would get £73.29 plus £5 worth of meals. In addition, E would pay no tax on the meals. Taking income tax into account as well, E takes home about £71 a week from the £80, or about £68 from the £77, plus getting the meals. H is no worse off, whilst E is about £2 better off each week.

Planning finances ahead

I expect, like me, you plan to retire sometime. How are you going to be able to afford it? If there are some years to go before you retire, be warned that the state pensions will be worth nothing like as much then as now. Why? The fact is that at and beyond the end of the century there will be more retired people, and fewer people at work paying NI contributions. So we cannot then afford the level of pensions we pay out now. The moral is simple: if you want a better standard of living than that, you must buy it in the meantime.

Think also what would happen if you were killed in an accident, or maimed so you could not carry on your business? Who would look after your wife/widow (it may be even worse for widowers) and any smaller children? Pensions for widows will be cut along with the retirement pension, and for the same unavoidable reason. Even now, are widow's pensions as good as your family's standard of living?

A personal pension

When starting a small business, and strapped for cash, financing pensions and insurance against person disaster looks like a luxury. In reality, it is a trade-off – earnings now or earnings then. What makes it a direct trade-off are the tax rules. If you pay money into an approved pension or assurance scheme, and you are either self-employed or your money is going into a personal pension, you get a tax deduction for the money going into the fund, and the fund pays no income tax or capital gains tax on its profits whilst the money is in the fund. You only pay when the money comes back out again as income – lump sums can be free of tax even then.

Pension funds can invest your money in safe investments on better terms than you can. Even a cautious start on a pensions policy will be something for which you are most grateful 20 years on. Get quotes on a self-employed pension scheme from insurance companies and brokers, and find out how much it will cost you. Payments are usually monthly, and can vary from year to year with the profits. Read **Personal Pensions** for a full account.

Life and health insurance

Think also what will happen to your business if you die or are unable to work any more. And if you are in business with partners or fellow directors of a company, what would happen if any of them suddenly died? Don't think it doesn't happen. Three years ago, I took over heading my department one Sunday because my predecessor had died without warning the previous afternoon.

If you are in a **partnership** just spare the time to think about what the death of a partner might mean. The loss of a close colleague could be bad enough if you merely think about the contribution they were making to the business. But on top of that, their dependants have the right to demand their share of the partnership – **in cash**. That could bring about the end of the partnership but, fortunately, it is possible to take out life assurance to cover this eventuality.

If you are a **company director**, you may have taken out loans and provided a personal guarantee that the loans will be repaid. If you die, your family could be left with a crushing burden with no way of repaying the debt. Loan insurance can protect them from that particular problem. In a small company, the death of a key person could destroy the business – or it could just dry up due to the loss of your top engineer or salesman. Key man insurance can provide the funds to cover the loss giving you the precious breathing space to recover and reorganise.

Besides life insurance, find out about **insurance against disability or ill-health**. Remember, once you are self-employed there is no big employer standing behind you to pay you whilst you get better. You can claim **state sickness benefit**, and should do so straight away if you are ill and off work, but that is only a small help. **Medical expenses insurance** will allow you more flexibility in getting treatment at times that affect your work less.

Business insurance

You can insure against almost any risk. As every major disaster shows, a large number of people assume it will never happen to them. It does. The trouble is, once it *has* happened, the financial problems of being uninsured may prevent them ever getting financially sorted out afterwards. What is more, you get full **tax relief** for all insurance premiums to protect the business – but you don't get full tax relief if you have to spend out money to replace something damaged in a disaster.

Before it happens to you, here is a checklist of kinds of insurance you should consider having. First, three forms of **compulsory insurance** – cover you must have:

- **Employer's liability insurance** – You must be insured against liability to any employee who is injured as a result of your carelessness, or that of any other employee. And you must display the insurance certificate at the workplace.
- **Road traffic insurance** – Your business vehicles must be insured for passenger and other third party cover.
- **Premises insurance** – Not required by law, but it is normally required either from a business tenant by a landlord, or by anyone lending money on the premises under a mortgage, to cover rebuilding costs from a fire or other disaster.

Other aspects of your business you should also consider insuring include:

- **Fire** – to cover the contents too
- **Special perils** – to cover things normally left out of fire policies, such as bursting water tanks
- **All risks** – to make your policy even wider than that, for example covering accidents
- **Theft** – from buildings or vehicles (other than shoplifting or by staff)

- **Money** – in buildings, on staff or otherwise
- **Goods in transit** – what happens if the delivery lorry crashes, or the post gets lost?
- **Business interruption** – not only is your building damaged by a fire, but you may also have to shut down for a period. Who pays the wages then?
- **Liability** – we've already covered employer's liability. There is also **public liability** (eg when a customer slips on your newly-washed shop floor and breaks a leg) and **product liability** (eg when due to a mistake in manufacture the clothes you sell irritate people's skins badly)
- **Engineering** – to cover breakdown of machinery, including computers
- **Credit** insurance against bad debts
- **Fidelity** – is aimed to protect you from dishonest employees
- **Legal expenses** – helps meet the legal costs bill if you get involved in legal actions
- **Travel** – when you are injured by accidents whilst travelling.

This checklist is taken from the **Small Business Advice Files** produced by the Association of British Insurers (address at end of book). Get a copy from them or from insurance companies or brokers and, once you have decided at what level you should be insuring each kind of risk, get quotes from a number of companies for that cover. Many companies sell packaged policies covering the needs of the average small business and that may suit you well, but also check whether you have special needs not covered by the usual policy.

Keep your policies under review

Once you have obtained insurance cover, you need to keep an eye on two aspects of the insurance. First, make sure you review the level of cover from time to time, both as values change and as your business grows, to ensure you remain fully insured. If you insure only half the value of the business, don't be surprised if the insurance company pay out only half your claim. The other point is to note the terms of the insurance policy, and any requirements imposed on you. Do you need to take certain safety measures to make a claim valid? Do thefts have to be reported promptly to the police? Is there a time limit within which claims must be made?

15 Being the boss

Firing staff is never fun. It is also expensive on your funds, time and standing with other employees. Not firing someone who ought to go is even more expensive. That is one reason why you should take great care to employ the right people for the right jobs. A better reason is that your staff are your best assets, and deserve and need the best management.

Let the person fit the job

When you need employees sort out three things before you appoint anyone:

- a **job description** for each job;
- the **terms and conditions** on which each job is offered;
- the **qualifications** needed by anyone holding the job.

Establish these first, and you are more likely to appoint, and keep, the right person.

Job descriptions

The clearer and better these are, the less room there is for staff to dispute what they are supposed to be doing. Work out your own standard document for all staff. Think about the following:

- Title of job
- Purpose of job
- Duties to be performed
- Special tasks assigned to job-holder
- Responsibilities of job-holder
- To whom job-holder answers
- Who answers to job-holder
- Authority of job-holder

Everyone should be given a job description at the start, and
the contents should be made clear during the appointing
process. That gives you both a point of reference. The
description also lets you think about what hours the job
requires. Do you want full-time staff? Part-time staffing may
give you more flexibility.

Terms and conditions

Decide what bargain you are striking for the job, and make
this clear to any appointee during the appointment – not
afterwards. Better still, write it down. The law requires you
to give an employee a statement of the terms of employment
within 13 weeks of starting with you, unless you have already
set all the terms out in writing. The statement must include
the following: job title; date job started; date employee first
worked for you; pay, and basis of calculation; hours of work;
holidays and entitlement to holiday pay; arrangements during
sickness, including sick pay; any pension; period of notice,
or length of employment if it is fixed term; procedure to deal
with grievances.

Generally, terms and conditions are for agreement between
you and each employee. In practice there are many limits to
this. Where the job is covered by a Wages Council, their
standard conditions apply. If there is an agreement between
employers federations and unions, you will probably want to
go along with that.

Legal requirements

All employees are entitled to minimum periods of notice and to be treated without racial or sexual discrimination, including equal pay for men and women doing work of equal value. Staff paying NI contributions are entitled to statutory sick pay and, in appropriate cases, statutory maternity pay, and may be entitled to maternity leave. Entitlement to some of these requirements only arise after employees have worked full-time for two years, or part-time for five years, and maternity leave can only be claimed if proper notice is given.

Under the 1986 Wages Act you must give staff a statement of how their pay is made up when paying them, including details of tax and other deductions. Fines or pay reductions, so far as permitted under that Act, must be agreed with the staff concerned. Staff are entitled to have safe working conditions. You can be liable in the criminal courts for failing to provide this. You should also ensure your premises comply with the standards of the Fire Precautions Act (check this with your local Fire Service). If you have more than four employees, you must adopt a written health and safety policy. The **Department of Employment**, the **Equal Opportunities Commission**, the **Commission for Racial Equality**, and the **Health and Safety Commission** all provide free leaflets setting out the requirements in some detail, and will offer further guidance.

Hiring the staff

Decide what are the minimum requirements for each job. Then you can set about finding the staff, making clear what is expected of them. You could use recruitment agencies, but they can be quite expensive, as can the long-term use of staff obtained through the 'temp' agencies – though for very short jobs that may be a good answer. Find out their rates before using them. For some jobs it may be better to use **sub-contractors** rather than hire your own staff. This may also save you having to buy expensive equipment or tools if the sub-contractor will supply these.

Hiring staff is still a remarkably hit-and-miss affair in most cases. For straightforward jobs this may not matter, if you are satisfied about the employee's basic abilities, but appointment of your senior manager on the basis of a short interview and shorter letter of application is decidedly risky. Take careful steps to get a broader picture by arranging more than one interview, getting references, making informal enquiries, and encouraging prospective employees to do the same. Use your interviews well, making sure you cover all the important points, and giving the candidate plenty of chance to talk. And treat the candidates well. Why create unnecessary enemies?

Helping staff

Too many employers assume, once a member of staff is appointed, that is that. Review the post on a continuing basis so the employee can, and wants to, give of his or her best to the business. Most people want both to work well and to know that they are doing so. They will get satisfaction out of doing a good job. It gives most people their identity. Think why you wanted to go into your business – was it dissatisfaction with your employer? Make sure, above all, you are a good boss, and your staff will repay your efforts.

Being a good boss depends partly on making clear to staff what is expected of them, and then – in a very positive way – appraising them fairly to see if they are doing this. They should be told on regular reviews – perhaps every year – how they are doing. If they are doing really well, they should be treated, and paid, accordingly. If not, they should be told clearly what is going wrong, and helped to put it right. Targets should be set and attainment rewarded. And don't skimp on the training. Above all, take them into your confidence so that they see what they are supposed to be doing. Managing staff well does not just happen – it needs planning, too, and an acceptance that the 'other side' is not another side at all. Your staff have the same broad feelings and attitudes as you.

Firing staff

Hopefully, if you planned your job descriptions right, and chose wisely, and then helped positively, not much of this needs to be done. If it does, follow a fair and thorough procedure, and the law will support you rather than hinder you. If not, you can be taken to the Industrial Tribunal for unfair dismissal. An employee cannot take you to an Industrial Tribunal until he or she has worked for you for two years (five years part-time). That gives you a period during which the employee's suitability can be assessed.

If staff are unsatisfactory, make sure they know why. Tell them why, pointing out the rules. It is good practice to give written warnings of this, and ask staff to sign copies to show they have received the warnings. But give them a chance to explain and see whether things can be improved by them and for them. Then give them a chance to sort things out. If you are still dissatisfied, give a second written warning, pointing out clearly the consequences if there is no improvement, and making sure they know what is required of them.

Giving notice

If after all this they still do not meet the requirements, give them proper notice under their contracts. Best practice will be to confirm this in writing, giving reasons for dismissal. If you follow a systematic and fair approach, there is little danger of your being found to have dismissed someone unfairly.

If someone has been in gross breach of his terms of employment – stealing from the business, physical violence on others at work or similar reasons – **instant dismissal** is probably fair. But make sure you have inquired into the circumstances, if you were not there at the time.

After employees leave

When staff leave, tell the tax authorities. If your employee claims social security, you will probably be asked why the job ended. If you say the job ended because the employee left voluntarily without good reason, or was fired because of misconduct, the employee may lose unemployment benefit for up to 26 weeks, and get only about half supplementary benefit during that period. This can be a severe penalty, so be fair on employees even after they have left.

If you are asked to give a **reference** for an ex-employee make sure it is honest. If it is too good and misleads a future employer, he could sue you for negligent misstatement. If it is deliberately and maliciously bad, the employee could sue you for defamation. If you do not wish to give a bad reference, it is better to stay silent.

16 Growing bigger

Businesses have life-spans like everything else, though the speed at which they grow up – and old – depends far less on nature than on those running them. Whatever uncertainties await, one thing is guaranteed. Once started, your business will never stand still. It will always be changing. Your job is to plan and manage that change, so the business goes on growing and renewing itself. To grow big is not of itself the aim. What is needed is a good cash-flow and growing profits. That can come two ways: increasing the **efficiency** of the business, and increasing its **scale**.

Make the business more efficient

At first, the main job of a business is to get going, to acquire customers as fast as possible to produce a positive cash-flow and then an operating profit. Hopefully, it will grow fast, but some activities will be more profitable than others. Once the business is going, growth amd profitability must be kept under review. Monitor profitability so that attention can be concentrated on the high-margin products, and monitor general business administration so excess general overheads can be trimmed.

The accounts and product costing should show where the high margin business is and also if any products sell at a loss. The customer 'bank' as it is sometimes called, also needs monitoring. Is there a particularly good group of customers emerging? If so, should your efforts be concentrated more on them? Should you be expanding the product range of those things which that sort of customer wants, whilst holding other sales more steady? Or are you, after an initial spurt, relying only on established customers, without sufficient new ones being introduced?

The point here is that market research is a continuing operation, not just a one-off. Whatever you do, the market will not stand still. Similarly, your advertising and selling effort needs assessing to see if it is supporting the most effective parts of the business, or parts needing boosting.

Let technology chip in

The other area to monitor is general overheads. It is a fundamental law of physics that order always degenerates into chaos. It applies to businesses as much as to atoms. Hence one of those laws attributed to Murphy: left to themselves, business costs always rise until they are overhead. The answer is constantly to reimpose order. One way the business can do this is to borrow the skills of the physicist, and get a computer in.

Computers and similar advances cannot be ignored. I said that in a previous book, when playing with my new (now almost worn out) little (I then thought it big) computer. This book is written on one that is immensely more powerful, but cost no more in real terms. What can it do? Any of the following:

- **word processor** (with a built-in spelling check and dictionary, and quite good enough to produce a news sheet without more).
- **spreadsheet** – an electronic worksheet which does the sums as you go along. Combined, the two are used to produce ready-made sets of **business accounts**.
- **database** – a highly efficient way of holding information,

ideal for holding mailing lists that can be used selectively. Information about or for customers can be stored for quick access. Computer-based stock-holding lists are also increasingly familiar.

- **graphics** – anything from the mock-up account book pages in this text to complicated CAD (computer-aided design for engineers and architects) applications.

Begin at the end

Don't get carried away with the computer as a new toy. Before you get one, check what precisely needs doing. The first stage of introducing a computer is **systems analysis** – and that can be done with advantage anywhere, even if you don't want a computer. This means analysing the system of work into each of its stages, to see what can be automated, and how. In theory, you then get the computer to do all those jobs which can be left to it.

In practice, things don't work like that. Specially written computer programmes can be enormously expensive, and full of teething problems and bugs. Being realistic, you need to find the **software** (as the programmes are universally called) to suit your business. There are an increasing number of sophisticated small business packages available combining, within limits, all the functions set out above. One problem is those limits. Nothing is worse than spending ages getting all your accounts transferred on to a computer, only to find a year later it is not big enough and you have to start again.

Only when you know you can get a software package that suits your needs should you then set about getting the **hardware** you need. This will include the computer itself, backed by a good memory capacity (hard disks are now so cheap relatively that they must be considered), a monitor (though I used our old television for ages, it was not so good on my eyes), and a printer. There are plenty of magazines that give you a good idea of current prices, which can be anything from a few hundred pounds (less tax relief) upwards. One other thing to look for is a system that will need the minimum time down – out of action – and that can be backed up, that is, you have a stand-by in case something goes wrong with it. You only find out by experience just how frustrating it is to wipe out a whole year's budget through some minor fault, only to discover you have no other copy. I have, and recommend you don't.

Properly used, a computer can speed up your accounting and clerical jobs, make your marketing information more usable, keep tabs on your stock and outstanding bills, improve the quality of your letters and publications and allow you to keep a tighter check on what is going on.

Get registered

If you use a computer to keep any information about anyone else (customers, mailing lists, employee files or other personal information), register under the Data Protection Act. Get in touch with the **Data Protection Registry** (address at end). They will send you the relevant forms and explanatory books. The Registry keeps a public register of all those with computer-based databanks of personal information. You may demand to see register entries, and can demand from anyone who is registered copies of any information held about you on the register. Small fees are payable both for registration and to get copies of information from a data holder.

Remember also that any of your customers or staff might demand information about themselves. If you keep staff references or confidential comments on customers on computer, you must be prepared to show it to them if asked. If you do not wish to do that, keep the information out of your computer's memory.

Expanding the business

Will only you know when the business is ready to expand? Well, no – you may be too near to it to see the obvious. The detached observer may be the best judge of this. Yet again, this is something on which to get the experts in. Don't forget you can go back to your local enterprise agency for help here either generally or to discuss what sort of expertise to tap. Your accountants, bankers and lawyers may all also have a role to play. The DTI's Enterprise Initiative is aimed at encouraging small businesses to seek expert advice – and will pay part of the bill.

Plans to expand involve reassessing the things looked at already in this book, but from a stronger base. Questions of location need reviewing, as will the business structure. If it is getting beyond one person, it needs to become at least a partnership or probably a company. It will also need recapitalising.

Expand from strength

Whilst there are many ways to expand, it is less risky to expand from strength. Your strength lies in your existing products and your existing customers, so the safe routes forward are to sell your present products to new customers or to sell new products to your existing customers. Of course, the bigger the product range and the larger your customer bank, the wider your range of options. But if you try selling a new product to a new customer, you are in uncharted waters. Even the biggest companies can lose their way doing this – smaller businesses can seldom afford the risk.

Another route forward is to buy someone else's product range and customers by acquiring or merging with another business. Aggressive expansion of businesses usually takes place through this route, perhaps to increase the national spread of a business, or to buy out a rival, or to diversify into a compatible area of business. This is often called 'horizontal' expansion. You can also aim to integrate your business 'vertically' that is, link all the stages of business from first production to final sale to customer. Manufacturers do this when they open up their own stores. Steps of this sort involve considerable cash allocations, and require expert advice. For example the major firms of accountants maintain a shared data bank of businesses for sale, so if looking to purchase a business, they can help in several ways.

Raising further cash

Raising money second time around may prove easier than at the start, if the business shows it knows what it is up to. It has the advantage of being able to produce accounts and balance sheets to show what has happened, and of being able to get capital from a wider range of sources, for both long-term and short-term funding.

If its plans are big enough, it will have access to the **venture capital** market of long-term funding, where there is a wide range of finance available either as loans, or for buying a share of the **equity** of the business, that is, become part owner by buying part of the company's share capital. This is a highly specialist field, and needs approaching through an advisor such as a banker or one of the major accountants with access to the necessary contacts, but the **British Venture Capital Association** (address at end of book) will give more details.

Other possibilities for short-term finance open up, as the company is a surer prospect. It can sell its debts. This is done by **factoring**, the process of getting a factor to collect your debts for you. The factor will advance you much of the money covered by the debts (perhaps 80%), at interest, and then collect the debts and account to you for the balance, less charges. Contact the **Association of British Factors** (address at end of book) to find out more.

Another method of freeing company cash resources is by **leasing** equipment rather than buying it. This involves the company arranging for a finance house to buy capital items on behalf of the business, and then renting the assets to the business. The company ties up no capital assets, but has instead a predictable revenue (and tax-deductible) expenditure over the useful life of the asset. The **Equipment Leasing Association** will provide further information (address at end).

Banks will remain major lenders to larger businesses, not least because they have their own venture capital branches. If your bankers have followed you loyally so far, they are not likely to desert you now! But there are many alternatives, and all should be investigated as indicated.

This list includes addresses of all organisations mentioned in the text and a selection of others. Lack of space prevents a fuller list, but inclusion or exclusion implies neither recommendation nor criticism. Get other addresses from your local reference library or the Small Firms Service. The list is organised in alphabetical order of the highlighted words (eg the British Overseas Trade Board is listed as British **Overseas Trade Board** under 'O'. This allows similar organisations to be listed together (see, eg, Accountants).

Accepting Houses Committee
Granite House
101 Cannon St
London EC4N 5BA

Institute of Chartered **Accountants in England and Wales**
Chartered Accountants Hall
PO Box 433
Moorgate Place
London EC2P 2BJ

Institute of Chartered **Accountants of Scotland**
27 Queen St
Edinburgh EH2 1LA

Chartered Association of Certified **Accountants**
29 Lincolns Inn Fields
London WC2A 3EE

Institute of Practitioners in **Advertising**
44 Belgrave Square
London SW1X 8QS

Advertising Standards Authority
Brook House
2–16 Torrington Place
London WC1E 7HN

British Steel (Industry)
2–6 Sydenham Road
Croydon
Surrey CR9 2LJ

Business in the Community
227a City Rd
London EC1V 1LX

Scottish **Business in the Community**
Eagle Star House
25 St Andrews Square
Edinburgh EH2 1AF

Association of British **Chambers of Commerce**
212 Shaftsbury Avenue
London WC2H 8EB

Companies Registration Office
ENGLAND AND WALES
Companies House
Crown Way
Maindy
Cardiff CF4 3UZ
N IRELAND
Dept of Economic Development
64 Chichester St
Belfast BT1 4JX
SCOTLAND
102 George St
Edinburgh EH2 3DJ

National Cooperative Development Agency
Broadmead House
21 Panton St
London SW1Y 4DR
and
Holyoake House
Hanover St
Manchester M60 0AS

CoSIRA
141 Castle St
Salisbury
Wiltshire SP1 3TP

Data Protection Registry
Springfield House
Water Lane
Wilmslow
Cheshire SK9 5AX

Design Council
28 Haymarket
London SW1Y 4SU

Disabled Living Foundation
346 Kensington High St
London W14 3NS

DTI (Dept of Trade and Industry)
1 Victoria St
London SW1H 0ET
Regional contacts for Enterprise Initiative:
Birmingham:
Ladywood House
Stephenson St
B2 4DT
Bristol:
The Pithay
BS1 2PD

Leeds:
Priestley House,
3–5 Park Row
LS1 5LF
Liverpool:
Graeme House
Derby Square
L2 7UP
London:
Ebury Bridge House
2–18 Ebury Bridge Rd SW1W 8QD
Manchester:
Sunley Tower
Piccadilly Plaza
M1 4BA
Newcastle-upon-Tyne:
Stanegate House
2 Groat Market NE1 1YN
Nottingham:
Severns House,
20 Middle Pavement
NG1 7DW
or telephone 0800 500 200

English Estates
St George's House
Kingsway
Team Valley
Gateshead NE11 0NA

Enterprise and Deregulation Unit
Dept of Employment
Caxton House
Tothill St
London SW1H 9HF

Equal Opportunities Commission
Overseas House
Quay St
Manchester M3 3HN

British **Exporters Association**
16, Dartmouth St
London SW1H 9BL

Office of **Fair Trading**
Bromyard Avenue,
Acton,
London W3 7BB

Headstart Marketing 40 Goodge St
London W1P 1FH

Highlands and Islands Development Board
Bridge House
27 Bank St
Inverness IV1 1QR

Hotel and Catering Training Board
International House
High Street
London W5

ICOF (Industrial Common Ownership Finance)
4 St Giles St
Northampton NN1 1AA

ICOM (Industrial Common Ownership Movement)
7 Corn Exchange,
Leeds LS1 7BP

In Business Now
Freepost London SW1E 5YZ

Association of **Independent Businesses**
Trowbray House
108 Weston St
London SE1 3QF

Confederation of British **Industry**
Centre Point
103 New Oxford St
London WC1A 1DU

Central Office of **Information**
Hercules Rd
London SE1 7DU

Instant Muscle
Haymill Centre
112 Burnham Lane
Burnham
Slough SL1 6LZ

British **Insurance Brokers Association**
BIBA House
14 Bevis Marks
London EC3A 7NT

Association of British **Insurers**
Aldermary House
Queen St
London EC4N 1TT

Ismaeli Business Information Centre
1 Cromwell Gardens
London SW7 2SL

The **Law Society**
113 Chancery Lane
London WC2A 1PL

Law Society of Scotland
26 Drumsheugh Gardens
Edinburgh EH3 7YR

Livewire
ENGLAND
Freepost, Newcastle upon Tyne NE1 1BR
N IRELAND
Freepost, Belfast BT7 1BR
SCOTLAND
Freepost, Newton Mearns, Glasgow G77 5BR
WALES
Freepost, Cardiff CF1 1YT

British Institute of **Management**
Management House
Cottingham Rd
Corby
Northants NN17 1TT

Institute of **Management Consultants**
32 Hatton Garden
London EC1

Institute of **Marketing**
Moor Hall
Cookham
Maidenhead
Berks SL6 9QH

Mid Wales Development
Ladywell House
Newtown
Powys SY16 1JB

Northern Ireland Dept of Economic Development
Aid to Industry Branch
22 Donegal St
Belfast BT1 2GP

Northern Ireland Local Enterprise Development Unit
LEDU House
Upper Galwally
Belfast BT8 4TB

The **Open University**
PO Box 76
Milton Keynes MK7 6AN

British **Overseas Trade Board**
1 Victoria St
London SW1

Chartered Institute of **Patent Agents**
Staple Inn Buildings
High Holborn
London WC1V 7PZ

The **Patent Office**
State House
66–71 High Holborn
London WC1R 4TP

Institute of **Patentees and Inventors**
Suite 505A
Triumph House
189 Regent St
London WIR 7WF

Production Engineering Research Association
Nottingham Rd
Melton
Leics LE13 0PB

Project Fullemploy
102 Park Village East
London SW1 3SP

Institute of **Purchasing and Supply**
Easton House
Easton on the Hill
Stamford
Lincs PE9 3NZ

Scottish Development Agency
120 Bothwell St
Glasgow G2 7JP

Scottish Industry Department (IDS)
Sandyford Rd
Paisley
Glasgow G2 6AT

National Federation of **Self-employed and Small Businesses**
32 St Annes Rd West,
Lytham St Annes
Lancs FY8 1NY

Small Business Bureau
32 Smith Square
London SW1 3HH

Small Firms Division, DTI
Steel House
Tothill St
London SW1H 9NF

Small Firms Service
Birmingham:
Alpha Tower
Suffolk St
Queensway B1 1TT
Bristol:
6th Floor
The Pithay
BS1 2NB
Cambridge:
Carlyle House
Carlyle Rd
CB4 3DN
Cardiff:
16 St Davids House
Wood St
CF1 1ER

Edinburgh:
Rosebury House
Haymarket Terrace EH12 5EZ
Glasgow:
21 Bothwell St
G2 6NR
Leeds:
1 Park Row
City Square
LS1 5NR
London:
Ebury Bridge House
2–18 Ebury Bridge Rd SW1W 8QD
Manchester:
3rd Floor
Royal Exchange Buildings
St Annes Square M2 7AH
Newcastle:
Centro House
3 Cloth Market
NE1 1EE
Nottingham:
Severns House
20 Middle Pavement
NG1 7DW
Reading:
Abbey House
Abbey Square
RG1 3BE
or telephone FREEFONE ENTERPRISE

British **Standards Institution**
2 Park St
London W1A 2BS

Business **Statistics Office**
Cardiff Rd
Newport
Gwent NP9 1XG

Department of Employment **Training Agency**
HEAD OFFICE:
Moorfoot
Sheffield S1 4PQ
REGIONAL OFFICES:
Basingstoke
Telford House
Hamilton Close
RG21 2UZ
Birmingham:
Alpha Tower
Suffolk St
Queensway B1 1UR
Bristol:
4th Floor
The Pithay BS1 2NQ
Cardiff:
4th Floor
Companies House
Crown Way
Maindy CF4 3UZ
Edinburgh:
9 St Andrews Square
EH2 2QX
Leeds:
Jubilee House
33–41 Park Place LS1 2RL
London:
236 Grays Inn Rd
WC1 8HN
Manchester:
Washington House
New Bailey St M3 5ER
Newcastle upon Tyne:
Broadacre House
Market St NE1 6HH
Nottingham:
2nd Floor
2 Clinton St East
N61 3QD

English **Tourist Board**
24 Grosvenor Gardens
London SW1W 0ET

Scottish **Tourist Board**
23 Ravelston Terrace
Edinburgh EH4 3EU

Welsh **Tourist Board**
Brunel House
2 Fitzalan Rd
Cardiff CF2 1UY

Welsh Development Agency
Pearl Building
Greyfriars Rd
Cardiff

Welsh Office Industry Department
Cathays Park
Cardiff CF1 3NQ

Women in Enterprise
26 Bond St
Wakefield
Yorks WF1 2QP

The Prince's **Youth Business Trust**
8th Floor
Melbury House
Melbury Terrace
London NW1 6LZ

after 15   June 1990 the address will be:
5 The Pavement
Clapham
London SW4 0HY

Regional Offices:
Bedfordshire/Herefordshire/Buckinghamshire (0707 271474)
Berkshire/Oxfordshire (0635 253069/523472)
Cambridgeshire (0223 63312)
Cheshire (0928 563037)
Cumbria (09467 71739/74980)
Derbyshire (0246 207379/208743, 0332 240644)
Devon & Cornwall (0752 767157)
Essex (0268 728078)
Gloucestershire (0452 307028)
Hereford & Worcester (0905 765489)
Humberside (0405 768229, 0482 27266)
Kent (0622 694280/694341)
Lancashire (0772 52166)
Leicestershire (0533 610080)
Lincolnshire (0522 531264)
London North (North West: 081 968 3713,
    North East: 071 247 4241)
London South (071 498 2774)
Manchester (061 872 0155, 0772 203575)
Merseyside (051 709 0185)
Norfolk (0603 6259877)
Northamptonshire (0536 513165)
North East (0388 420042/605265, 091 510 9191)
Nottinghamshire (0602 484619)
Shropshire (0743 252593)
Southern Counties (0703 256240/1, 081 397 5141,
    071 821 4153)
Staffordshire (0543 253622)
Suffolk (0502 563286, 0728 642139)
Surrey (0784 244558)
Western Counties (0272 252012)
West Midlands (021 236 3902/5095, 0743 275000)
Yorkshire North (0904 624835, 0947 87365)
Yorkshire South (0302 731228)
Yorkshire West (0532 626333, 0274 391186, 0484 432999)
Wales North (0352 710444)
Wales South & West (0685 882515, 0222 551846,
    0446 733886)
Northern Ireland (0232 328000)

Endnote

You have been asked lots of searching questions, had your motives questioned, and been given plenty to do through this book. Two messages have been repeatedly put to you – think and plan ahead, and get the experts in. Indeed, you may be wondering why you need a guide if you end up asking an expert anyway. That's quite simple. You should be paying experts to answer your questions, not to ask them. The best advice is usually given to the client who knows exactly what is wanted. If you think through all the issues raised in this book, and seek help where it is suggested, your business will be off to a sound start. And I wish you all success.

I have tried in writing the book to practise what I am asking you also to practise, and therefore resisted at the beginning any personal account or history of this work. But it would be churlish and bad manners not to include even at the end of the book a note of my very genuine and grateful thanks to many people.

Just as you are asked to, I have brought in the experts, asked my family and friends what they thought, phoned FREEFONE ENTERPRISE and the Enterprise Initiatives, sent for the publications . . .

My warmest thanks to all who have helped, wittingly or unwittingly, and in particular my brother Bryan and others of my family, my friends and colleagues, not least my secretary and other colleagues at the Centre for Commercial Law Studies, and those at Allied Dunbar, BAT Industries, Business in the Community and the Swindon Enterprise Trust, the Law Society and Longman, who have advised, encouraged, warned and assisted. They have been concerned that the accumulated wisdom about past mistakes should be as available as possible to you, to try and stop you repeating the bad parts of history and encourage you to repeat the good parts. Warm thanks also to the reviewers, correspondents, buyers and borrowers of the previous editions. Above all, my thanks to Lis, Richard, Edward and Thomas for tolerating my repeated desertion of their company for that of the green screens, and for providing that support which I urge you to gain.

In updating this book, I must repeat my thanks for the support and help from those who contributed their time and expertise to this and the previous edition, particularly my Secretary Sandra Baird. Times are tougher in the early 90's than they were a few years ago, making the need to plan all the more important. Again, I wish you success.

Charlbury, Oxfordshire   David Williams
March 1990

Index

Other titles in this series